Creatively Financing and Resourcing Catholic Schools

Conversations in Excellence

edited by Regina Haney and Joseph O'Keefe, SJ

A Component of SPICE: **S**elected **P**rograms for **I**mproving **C**atholic **E**ducation, a national diffusion network for Catholic schools

National Catholic Educational Association

Copyright 1999 National Catholic Educational Association
1077 30th Street, NW, Suite 100
Washington, DC 20007-3852
ISBN 1-55833-233-2

Design: Center for Educational Design and Communication, Washington, DC
Cover Photos: Saint Philip the Apostle School, Dayton Catholic Elementary School,
and the Alliance for Catholic Education: University of Notre Dame.

Contents

Chapter 1

Overview of SPICE 1998

– Carol Cimino, SSJ; Regina M. Haney; Joseph M. O'Keefe, SJ

Selected Programs for Improving Catholic
Education (SPICE) was created in 1996 to assist
Catholic school leaders to choose and to replicate
programs that ingeniously and successfully meet
the needs of the contemporary Catholic school.
SPICE is a Catholic diffusion network cosponsored
by Boston College and the National Catholic
Educational Association. Its purpose is to identify
and validate successful programs, and to assist
other Catholic elementary schools, secondary
schools and diocesan offices to adapt them.

At the annual meeting of SPICE, called
Conversations in Excellence, educators with

exemplary programs share their successes with other practitioners, Catholic school administrators, professors from Boston
College and experts from around the country. Each year's program has a specific focus: in 1996 it was "Integrating the
Mission" and in 1997 it was "Creatively Meeting the Needs of
Children and Their Families." These conferences have led to
two publications thus far:

- Regina Haney and Joseph O'Keefe, SJ. *Conversations in
  Excellence: Integrating Mission.* Washington, DC:
  National Catholic Educational Association, 1997.
- Regina Haney and Joseph O'Keefe, SJ. *Conversations in
  Excellence: Providing for the Diverse Needs of Youth and
  Their Families.* Washington, DC: National Catholic
  Educational Association, 1998.

The focus in 1999 is "Forming Innovative Learning
Environments through Technology" and in 2000 it will be
"Integrating the Social Teachings of the Church into Catholic
Schools."

At the 1998 Conversations in Excellence conference, titled
"Creatively Financing and Resourcing Catholic Schools," ten
teams from across the country gathered with university faculty,
superintendents and other experts in the field to share their
knowledge and to develop a process for assisting others to
replicate or adapt the exemplary programs.

Featured as keynote speaker was Peter Lynch, vice chairman
and trustee of Fidelity Management and Research Company,
who has taken a leadership position in raising scholarship
money for Catholic school students in the Archdiocese of
Boston. Lynch discussed[1] different approaches to seeking donations from corporations and philanthropists, making the point
that the value of Catholic schools is underrated. He also spoke
of the need for education in a job market that is requiring
more skills than in the past. He pointed out that people often
think Catholic schools have high entrance standards and students who misbehave are easily expelled. "There is no admission standard. We take every kid." Through research, Lynch
said, he learned that significant discipline problems are typically
nonexistent in Catholic schools. He attributed this to the fact

that Catholic schools have an added dimension to their curriculum. "Everyone knows what the three R's are, but in Catholic schools there are three other R's as well—respect, responsibility and religion."

Lynch said that people often assume the term "dropout" means "high school dropout." As a result, scholarship money is available only for older children who are perceived to be in need. But there are a number of children who can't make it through elementary school.

"There's money out there for college, but there's no money to go to third grade. All the money out there is meaningless to someone who can't get through grammar school."

Lynch told the assembly that when seeking corporate gifts, an active, persistent philosophy works best. "Don't do it with a letter. Meet with them face-to-face even if it means waiting six months," he urged, making the point that it is much easier for a potential donor to decline in a letter; in a meeting it will be more difficult to do so. He also warned against meeting with corporate "giving officers" instead of top executives. "That's a euphemism. They're there to say no." Lynch said that when seeking funds it is important to refrain from criticizing public education.

Lynch also discussed some of the strategies he has implemented with the Inner-City Scholarship Fund—a program that raised $3.2 million for students in the Archdiocese of Boston last year. "It's easier to raise money for scholarships," he declared. "That way people won't think their donation will be spent on salaries or the leaky roof." He supported the effective tactic used by the ICSF: create an interaction between donors and children. "The most effective thing we do is get the children to write letters to givers," he said. "Getting five or six notes from kids means a lot." Another tactic Lynch discussed was the annual bus tour he takes with potential donors to an inner-city school. "If you can get donors to see the school, then you've got them," he emphasized. Lynch spoke of poor communities where students are so eager to be in school that they are visibly saddened on Fridays because they won't be in school over the weekend. "People aren't ready for that."

Lynch told the audience that donors should be made to understand that education benefits society as a whole and that everyone has a vested interest in keeping children in schools. He reminded the conference that 20 years ago it was much easier to find a job with little or no schooling but today, with technology doing the simple jobs, education is essential. As an example of changing job requirements, Lynch used military service. While a blood test was once the only requirement for admittance, today there is an aptitude test which half of all applicants fail. "There are no jobs now for people without education. The point is we have a fabulous story that people have to hear."

As a result of the four-day event, it is hoped that the fabulous stories will be circulated widely. Ten programs are accessible for adaptation. These were showcased at the 1999 NCEA convention, are listed in the annual *SPICE Catalogue* and are posted on the NCEA Web site to facilitate communication with the programs' contact people.

Overview of *Creatively Financing and Resourcing Catholic Schools: Conversations in Excellence*

The ten exemplary SPICE programs are a central focus of this book. In chapter two, Carol Cimino, SSJ, director of the Catholic School Administrators Association of New York State, presents each of the ten programs. She describes the programs, articulates their goals, outlines their activities and discusses issues of implementation and adaptation.

The rest of the book contains material from the symposium's speakers. In chapter three, Joseph Claude Harris, consultant and noted expert on Catholic school finance, offers his overview of the current fiscal state of schools and his assessment of their chances for survival in the future. In the fourth chapter, Dale McDonald, PBVM, director of public policy and education research at NCEA, delineates funding opportunities from government and corporate sources. Mary Tracy, SNJM, of the Department of Secondary Schools at NCEA, describes successful school-based institutional advancement efforts in the fifth chapter. In chapter six, Dr. Francis Butler, president of Foundations and Donors Interested in Catholic Activities (FADICA), brings to light the perspectives of the philanthropic community, especially those organizations that have a special interest in church-related schools. In chapter seven, Joseph O'Keefe, SJ, associate professor of education at Boston College, examines the impending teacher shortage in the United States and its impact on Catholic schools. Lee Brennan, Lawrence Callahan and Regina Haney discuss the crucial role of the board in financing and resourcing the school in the eighth chapter. In chapter nine, Howard Gray, SJ, director of the Center for Ignatian Spirituality at Boston College, reminds his readers of the need to maintain a spiritual focus in the midst of fiscal concerns. Finally, a panel of five diocesan superintendents (Robert Bimonte, FSC, of Buffalo; Timothy Dwyer of Rochester; Jerome Porath of Los Angeles; Ann Dominic Roach, OP, of Boston and Michael Skube of Charlotte) and Lourdes Sheehan, RSM, then executive director of the Department of Chief Administrators of Catholic Education at NCEA, offer their perspectives on crucial issues of financing and resourcing.

Selected Programs for Improving Catholic Education could not exist without the efforts of many generous people. With gratitude, a list of acknowledgements and sponsors is located at the end of the book.

[1] Adapted from Stephen Gawlik, "Lynch Addresses NCEA Conference on Catholic School Financing," *The Pilot*, Washington, DC, July 17, 1998.

Chapter 2

Model Programs: Creatively Financing and Resourcing Catholic Schools

–Carol Cimino, SSJ

The 1998 focus area, "Creatively Financing and Resourcing Catholic Schools," lent itself to a variety of plans and programs designed to support Catholic schools. The focus area was not limited to programs that merely supply financial help to the schools; it also included those programs that provide human resources.

In addition, the 1998 programs included many more diocesan-wide plans, and plans that involve people other than those directly connected to the schools. In this sense, the public benefit of Catholic schools was emphasized and highlighted. Moreover, the term "creative" was certainly the watchword, as schools and dioceses came up with ingenious ways to solve the problem of supporting the schools.

Alliance for Catholic Education (ACE)
The University of Notre Dame, Notre Dame, Indiana

Program Description

Professional teaching is the first pillar of ACE. From the outset, ACE has held that its teachers must be prepared for the rigors of classroom teaching. Their two-year service commitment is grounded in an innovative teacher-training program that culminates in a Master of Arts in Teaching (MAT) degree from the University of Portland. During 16 weeks of training over two summers, ACE teachers serve with pay as instructors in the remedial, enrichment and bilingual classes of the South Bend public and diocesan schools in the morning. They integrate their experiences with the best available educational theory during graduate classes taught by Portland faculty on the Notre Dame campus in the afternoon. After completing each summer's training experience, ACE teachers travel to the parochial school systems of the South and Southeast. There, they teach full time in schools that report a chronic shortage of well-trained teachers, especially in math, science, the social sciences and theology.

Program Goals

In the life of each local community, ACE participants are invited to develop their own personal spirituality in the context of community, and to share with one another the journey of becoming committed Catholic school teachers. Given this program goal, ACE staff strive to provide ACE teachers with the tools to become professional educators and people of faith. ACE conducts five annual retreats in which the entire ACE cohort comes together to celebrate and to reflect on their lives and work.

Program Activities

ACE places great emphasis on supporting its teachers through the challenges and rewards of beginning teaching. Faculty supervisors formally observe each ACE teacher once per semester and maintain close contact with the new teachers through regular e-mail correspondence and reviews of classroom videos submitted each semester. In addition, newly trained teachers are paired with an experienced mentor teacher in the school where they serve. This professional mentorship is augmented by the peer support ACE teachers gain by living together in community. The program offers a series of evening workshops during the summer session, as well as two workshops/retreats during the regular school year, to provide participants with the skills to live a healthy community life. ACE staff members also visit each community to offer support and facilitate a solution to any difficulties that may arise. Finally, local diocesan resource people and Notre Dame alumni club members are present to welcome the ACE teachers to their local communities.

Implementation/Adaptation

ACE teachers are welcomed throughout the Southern dioceses of the United States. Superintendents of these dioceses demonstrate a need for ACE teachers, in accordance with ACE goals. Superintendents and the local community then provide specific resources, such as housing, for the ACE teachers during their time of service.

Many Catholic colleges, dioceses and religious orders have begun volunteer programs for young professionals interested in being of service to the Church, particularly in the area of Catholic education. Persons interested in either ACE teachers or ACE volunteers should contact the sponsoring agencies.

Catholic School Development Indianapolis-Style *(a series of programs)*
Archdiocese of Indianapolis, Office of Catholic Education, Indianapolis, Indiana

Catholic School Development Indianapolis-Style is not a single project, but a series of interrelated projects completed over a period of years, and designed to enhance the position of Catholic schools in the Archdiocese of Indianapolis. Five major projects are included in this story of a comprehensive archdiocesan approach to development.

It would be a mistake, however, to think that these programs or any other programs will be as successful as they might be without a strong vision and belief in Catholic schools and a commitment to a comprehensive program of institutional advancement and professional development. The success Indianapolis has had, as illustrated in these programs, is due mainly to an overarching vision and belief that Catholic schools are the most effective means to help parents pass on the faith, evangelize and address social inequities. Moreover, the arch-diocesan leadership in making a commitment to preserve and advance the mission of Catholic Education is also committed to some foundational principles. They are:

1. to assure quality Catholic education by teaching to high standards, measuring results and ensuring the Catholicity of our schools;

2. to provide excellent leadership and management for Catholic schools including planning, well-defined gover-nance and administrative structures, quality personnel, good business management and accountability; and

3. to provide a comprehensive approach to development that includes marketing, student recruitment, communi-cation, public relations, annual fund-raising, major gifts, capital campaigns, planned giving and endowments, pro-fessional development offices, etc.

Because these multiple projects designed for implementation from the diocesan level did not fit easily into the SPICE applica-tion format, each project was profiled separately, following as closely as possible the SPICE application questions.

Component1: School Marketing Efforts of the Archdiocese of Indianapolis, 1988–1995

Program Goals

The goal of this program was to reverse a 25-year enrollment decline in the elementary and high schools of the Archdiocese of Indianapolis and to increase student enrollment as rapidly as possible through joint marketing efforts. This program is a good example of creative financing and resourcing of Catholic education in that it involves mobilization of local school resources from the archdiocesan level and working together to do things that no one school could accomplish alone. It also involves community and business partnerships.

Program Activities

In 1988–1989, the Archdiocese of Indianapolis launched its first joint school marketing effort entitled "The Yellow Brick Road." This was a commercially-developed program with a "tool box" notebook of marketing ideas to be implemented locally. Regional training sessions were held for local Yellow Brick Road committees. Local effort was supplemented by archdiocesan-wide efforts, including radio and newspaper advertising, bill-boards, extensive direct mail, etc. The program started with a diocesan matching grant to subscribing schools. This effort for elementary schools, along with a similar "future quest" effort for the six interparochial high schools, was run for three years.

In 1990, Mr. Patrick J. Rooney, chairman of the board of the Golden Rule Insurance Company, was approached about sponsorship of the marketing efforts for Catholic schools. One year later he offered to support, redesign and help deliver the school marketing efforts. In addition to his personal donation of $55,000 a year for four years, he provided the auspices of the corporate advertising department of the Golden Rule Insurance Company which produced videos, high-grade advertising materials, radio and TV spots, direct mail pieces, training programs, etc., in conjunction with the Office of Catholic Education.

Simultaneously with the Advance Marketing Program, a program of "Incentive Grants to Open New Classrooms" was offered for three years. Based roughly on the idea from the movie, "Field of Dreams"—"Build it and they will come"—money was solicited from private donors to help reduce the financial risk for schools in opening new classrooms. Through a simple process, schools could apply for incentive grants of from $1,000 to $5,000 on the condition that they use the money to increase student capacity in their schools.

Component 2: The Comprehensive Development Project for Six Interparochial High Schools, 1994–1997

Program Description

In 1993, the Office of Catholic Education Development Team wanted to hire a fund-raising consultant to assist the six interparochial high schools with their fledgling development efforts.

All but one of the schools was significantly below national expectations for the amount raised through development efforts. Catholic School Management, Inc. was retained as project consultant. Instead of just focusing on fund raising, they recommended that the schools focus simultaneously on administrative and governance restructuring and a comprehensive approach to development, including marketing: public relations, good business practices, student recruitment, communications, annual funding, special events, endowments and planned giving. The methodology employed placed expert consultants in each school building in areas of administration and development over a period of three years. Progress was mentored step-by-step by the consultants and team, and progress was meticulously documented against the objectives of the archdiocesan strategic plan for schools and the strategic plans and comprehensive development plans developed by each of the schools. Both subjective/qualitative and objective/measurable objectives were monitored throughout the course of the project.

Program Goals

The goal of the Comprehensive Development Project was to "change the culture" within the six interparochial high schools of the Archdiocese of Indianapolis to one that supported comprehensive and effective development programs. This program is a good example of creative financing and resourcing of Catholic education in that it resulted in significant increases in involvement and gift revenue for the schools, and the process can be replicated in both elementary and secondary schools. It is also a good example of diocesan-local cooperation toward goals that would be difficult for any one school to meet alone.

Program Activities

1. By the end of the three-year consultation, five out of six high schools had adopted the president/principal model for administration and all six governance boards were restructured into trustee boards of limited jurisdiction. Three-year strategic plans were developed and implemented, comprehensive development plans were written and followed, special-event fund raising was greatly strengthened, restricted annual giving (scholarship funds) were started and growing, all schools were planning for

needed capital improvements, endowments were established at all six schools, comprehensive communication plans were in place with regular publication schedules, enrollment management and marketing programs were reorganized and strengthened, and guidance programs were strengthened as critical programs to the success of the schools.

2. The development of human resources to support the mission is one of the major goals of development and the absolute key to financial success as well. The major accomplishment of this project was in involving large numbers of parents and other supporters directly in the mission of the schools as new board members, development leaders, campaign solicitors or donors. In all of these areas, participation (and thus, ownership) was increased significantly. Just six volunteers were involved in development in 1993; 746 in 1997.

3. The Office of Catholic Education Development Team has now assigned a consultant from the office to take the place of the CAM consultants. Using what was learned through the project the diocese is designing a similar consulting program to assist the elementary schools with development.

Program Implementation

This type of program can be implemented by any type of school listed. However, economies of scale and future replication are best achieved in a joint effort led at the diocesan level.

Component 3: The Making a Difference Campaign for Indianapolis Center-City Schools, 1995–1998

Program Description

In 1994, newly installed Archbishop Daniel Buechlein made a public commitment to keep the eight center-city schools in Indianapolis open and viable. He vowed to do this through a partnership of parishes, parents, the greater archdiocesan community and the corporate community in Indianapolis. The Making a Difference Campaign was the first approach of the archdiocese to corporations.

Early research indicated that many corporate executives were unaware of the contributions made by Catholic center-city schools, unaware of the diverse populations served and, in some cases, unaware that the schools existed. Therefore, the archbishop commissioned a blue ribbon panel of archdiocesan officials and corporate leaders to write a white paper on the contributions of the center-city Catholic elementary schools. This document was used as a case to approach corporations about investing in the center-city schools.

For the first time, many high level corporate and civic leaders became involved in these efforts, including the mayor of Indianapolis and the president of Fifth Third Bank, who served as campaign chairperson. Initial major gifts were solicited and a corporate kick-off breakfast was held to which most of the city's corporate leaders were invited. Numerous tours of center-city schools were held in the next few weeks. Solicitors from the corporate community made calls on corporate leaders, along with archdiocesan officials.

A victory luncheon was held for donors at one of the center-city schools at the end of the campaign. Donors' names were published in a local business newspaper and a plaque was delivered to each major donor.

Program Goals
The goals of the archdiocesan "Making a Difference" campaign was to involve the Indianapolis corporate community in the future of Catholic education in the eight Indianapolis center-city Catholic schools and to provide significant financial aid for students attending these schools. The campaign is a good example of taking the cumulative needs of a group of schools and presenting them together as a very strong case for corporate support of alternative education in the inner-city. It was classic development.

Program Activities
Catholic school parents with contact in the corporate community were instrumental in making the campaign successful. Center-city parents were held to their end of the partnership in meeting their share of the tuition obligation. Many parents also testified about their satisfaction with Catholic schools in campaign literature and during visits to the schools.

Program Implementation

1. Staff development was not part of this program except that center-city school faculty members were made aware of the workings of the campaign and their contribution to it in the larger educational picture. Training for campaign solicitors was provided.

2. Corporate involvement and dollars are probably only significantly available to Catholic schools in areas where large numbers of non-Catholic and minority parents are served and the corporate community is well aware of the importance of alternative educational opportunities to urban public schools. Companies become involved because of the perceived necessity of these schools in anchoring urban communities.

Component 4: The Celebrating Catholic School Values Dinner, 1996 to Present

Program Description

Primarily a "friend-raiser," the Celebrating Catholic School Values Dinner also has been very successful as a fund raiser. The first year, all tables were sold out at $1,500 apiece and more than 1,100 people attended. There were four $15,000 corporate sponsors who covered the costs of the event. More than $100,000 for student financial aid was realized after event expenses were paid.

Program Goals

1. The major goal of the first Celebrating Catholic School Values Dinner in January 1996 was to build upon the work done in the "Making a Difference" campaign to involve the Indianapolis corporate and civic community with Catholic schools. In the second year, corporations throughout the 39 county archdiocese were approached for their support.

2. A second goal was to honor some outstanding Catholic school graduates and to tell the great story of Catholic schools through their life stories.

3. A final goal was to provide financial aid assistance to Catholic school families.

Program Activities

The Celebrating Catholic School Values Dinner was modeled on a similar event held annually in the Archdiocese of Louisville. It was conceived as a "friend-raiser" in the corporate community to raise awareness about Catholic schools in the Indianapolis community. Students served as ushers, and musical groups from a number of schools provided entertainment.

Corporate leaders were involved in direct leadership and solicitation for the campaign. The chairperson was the president/CEO of Allison Engine and the vice-president/CFO of the company served as co-chair of the steering committee, taking a very hands-on approach. More than 200 nominations were received and five outstanding Catholic school graduates and one community leader were honored. The speaker was former secretary of education, Dr. William Bennett. The mayor of Indianapolis and the governor of Indiana attended, along with many other dignitaries.

The second year, January 1997, the event had to be moved to a larger site because the original site to meet the demand. The president and CEO of Thomson Consumer Electronics, Inc. (RCA, GE, ProScan) served as chairperson. Corporations throughout the archdiocese were approached and all schools in the archdiocese were involved. Ambassador Alan Keyes, a Catholic school graduate, was the speaker. Five additional graduates were honored, including the current attorney general of Indiana, Pam Carter, the first African-American woman to hold this post in the nation. The distribution of financial aid was extended to high schools and grade schools throughout the archdiocese.

Program Implementation

1. Staff development consisted mainly of making school staff aware of the need for such an event and ensuring their participation. Volunteer input consisted of developing and working the event plan, assisting in the recruitment of high-level leadership, assisting and identifying gift prospects and award nominees, communicating about the event, soliciting gifts, evaluating the event and distributing the proceeds.

2. Although some of the private high schools in the archdiocese host events of a similar scale, this type of event
works best on the diocesan level, especially for elementary schools. It brings the schools together in a common
effort, it speaks to the excellence of the schools and it
allows all schools to share the spotlight. It is not, however, a substitute for the kinds of special events that each
school should sponsor as part of its development efforts.

Component 5: Building Communities of Hope Corporate Campaign, 1998–1999; Legacy of Hope Archdiocesan Capital Campaign, 1998–1999

Program Description

The Journey of Hope 2001 is an archdiocesan-wide effort initiated by Archbishop Daniel Buechlein which focuses on spiritual
renewal, evangelization and stewardship. The Legacy of Hope
is one aspect of this Journey.

The campaign is an effort to reach out to over 200,000
Catholics in the archdiocese, to increase stewardship to parishes
and the archdiocese and to raise $40 million for parish, school
and archdiocesan capital and endowment needs. Sixty percent
of the gifts will go directly to the parishes and 40% to archdiocesan needs, such as interparochial high schools, Catholic
Charities, etc. The public phases of the campaign will be conducted in all parishes during 1998. A campaign program is
being developed in each of the 150 parishes (including Catholic
elementary schools), each with its own unique case for support.
The archbishop's education secretary and other archdiocesan
leaders are involved in direct gift solicitation.

In the fall of 1997, the Lilly endowment announced an unprecedented $15 million matching gift to the private schools of
Marion County, Indiana (Indianapolis). This included a $5 mil-
lion gift to the Indianapolis Catholic schools to be administered
by the archdiocese. The match for these funds will be raised
mainly through the Legacy of Hope and Building Communities
of Hope campaigns.

Some specific objectives of the Building Communities of Hope
campaign are to replace two aging center-city Catholic school

buildings, to purchase a larger public school building for one of the eight and to refurbish the others, and to provide at least $9 million in endowment funds for student financial aid to replace the proceeds of the Making a Difference campaign. The case is once again being made to the corporate community. Local and national corporate leadership is involved.

Program Activities

A series of informational luncheons are being hosted by the center-city schools and individual major gift calls are being made to every major corporation in the city of Indianapolis. The purpose of the national focus is to make this a model for other inner-city fund raising efforts for Catholic schools.

Program Implementation

Staff development is not part of this program except that center-city school faculty members were made aware of the workings of the campaign and their contribution to it in the larger educational picture. Training for campaign solicitors has been provided by professional fundraisers.

The Building Communities of Hope campaign could be adapted by any diocese that has a large urban population to serve and that has a track record of previous cultivation and involvement of the corporate and business community.

Stewardship—A Way of Life

Catholic Diocese of Wichita, Wichita, Kansas

Program Description

1. In 31 of 32 parishes, no elementary school tuition is charged to parents who are active parishioners. Instead, the parish funds the school through its Sunday stewardship collection.

2. In all but a handful of situations, parishes also fund the high school tuition for active parishioners through the Sunday collection.

3. All parishes with students in high school also pay a direct assessment based on parish income, debt and location. In Wichita, this amounts to more than $2,000,000 for the two high schools. In Hutchinson, direct assessment and tuition are divided by the three parishes, based on the parish's ability to pay.

4. Parishes define "active parishioner" in different ways. Most require that the families make and keep a good faith pledge. In addition, many others make some effort to monitor time and talent commitments, Mass attendance, previous provisions for religious education, etc. [For example, St. Francis of Assisi Parish in Wichita has 2,500 member families and an average Sunday collection of $80,000, or about $4,000,000 a year. Of this amount, the parish funds a grade school of 775 students at a cost of about $2,200 per student; 250 students in the diocesan high schools at a cost of $2,400 per student; and a $275,000 direct assessment. The Parish's United Catholic Stewardship (cathedraticum) is 10% of all income.]

5. Although the specific application of these principles may be uneven, parishes, in general, focus much attention on the spirituality of stewardship. The success of this approach depends on maintaining stewardship as a life-long habit, well after children leave the school system. If stewardship is seen by the parents only as indirect tuition, the program will ultimately fail.

6. Since a person's pledge is based on income and personal level of commitment, low-income families are not hindered from receiving a Catholic education.

Program Goals

1. Establish stewardship as a diocesan culture which bonds parishioners to their faith, through their parish.

2. Bond parish and school together so that every Catholic school student must have an indissoluble relationship to his/her parish.

3. Instill in all parishioners a sense of responsibility for helping to fund all parish programs, including Catholic schools.

4. Make Catholic education available to all active Catholics, regardless of income, location, or ethnic group.

Program Activities

1. The bishop made a personal commitment to incorporate stewardship into the decision-making philosophy of the entire diocesan operation in 1985.

2. The entire month of November is set aside for stewardship renewal throughout the diocese. The renewal is led by a personal appeal from the bishop. The diocese provides motivational materials. Emphasis is on stewardship of time and talents, because if a person is generous with these, she/he will be generous with treasure.

3. The diocesan director of stewardship and other officials are available to assist parishes in incorporating stewardship concepts.

4. The diocese hosts an annual Stewardship Conference to re-teach basic concepts of stewardship. The diocese also publishes a stewardship manual.

5. Financial stewardship in the diocese is defined by the diocese as a goal of 8% of one's income to the parish and 2% for other charities.

6. A diocesan stewardship curriculum—Young Stewards in Action—is taught in all schools and religious education programs in November.

7. The Cathedraticum system is restructured so that parishes tithe an annual 10%. No annual diocesan appeals are held. No national collections are taken. Diocesan offices do not charge fees for their services.

8. The diocese formally discourages the use of tuition in the school system.

9. Even the current capital campaign is presented in stewardship terms as a "stewardship of assets."

Program Implementation

1. *Prayer and Reflection* A great deal of prayer and reflection are needed at all levels (diocesan, parish, etc.) for which stewardship is considered. Stewardship as a way of life is a radical departure from the tuition-subsidy approach of the past and requires extensive consideration of all the ramifications. Stewardship is a style of Christian spirituality, and not a way to fund schools.

2. *Planning* The Diocese of Wichita spent two years studying this process and revising its own internal processes. If stewardship is to be a way of life and not an effort to make tuition tax-deductible, sound and honest business practices are essential.

3. *Communication/Inservice* The following persons need to be involved:
   a. Diocesan leadership and agency heads
   b. Pastors and parish leadership
   c. School leadership and educators
   d. Parishioners
   e. Parents
   f. Students

4. *Adaptations* In a stewardship parish, focus shifts from individual resources to parish resources. The chief variables in determining parish resources are average family income and parish size. The diocese conducts no annual appeals and provides no subsidy to elementary schools. In a general way, the following suggestions should be considered:
   a. A parish of fewer than 300 families will have difficulty maintaining a nine classroom K-8 school relying on stewardship alone
   b. A parish of fewer than 600 families will have difficulty maintaining both an elementary school and paying tuition for all its Catholic high school students.
   c. A parish of fewer than 600 families with more than 35% of its families qualifying for free or reduced lunch will struggle to fund an elementary school and the parish.

WIN Schools *(Wegman Inner-city Voucher Program)*
Rochester Diocesan Office, Rochester, New York

Program Description
Over a period of several years, Mr. Robert Wegman, owner of a nationally ranked chain of supermarkets in the Northeast, made a series of gifts to the Catholic schools of the Rochester Diocese, specifically to sustain and increase the opportunities for inner-city youngsters to receive a Catholic education. Both Mr. and Mrs. Wegman continue to give personal attention to these schools and their students.

The WIN Program has helped to increase enrollment (K-6 grades) and guarantee, to an extent, retention in our city schools. The monies have provided for the hiring of an assistant superintendent for the six schools who would support the six principals in varied ways: facilitate collaboration in academic development, public relations and budgeting efforts; begin and maintain a volunteer program; and further parish support.

The assistant superintendent also serves as the school visitor to each school attending to curriculum, personnel and the school culture. The assistant superintendent is the coordinator for the WEE (Wegman Early Education, a pre-school program) and meets monthly with the WEE program coordinators. She also is the liaison to the City School District, School Health Advisory Board and City Planning Advisory Board.

Educational programs continue to be developed—volunteer programs, parish partnerships with each city school and a sub-urban parish, and an increase in the number of school advo-cates are in process.

The monies also support a school advocate supervised by the assistant superintendent and school principal. The advocate is a school psychologist who 1) serves as a listener and counselor for students, 2) supports students and parents and makes referrals for further academic needs or services and 3) provides inservice for parents and faculty. The advocate relates to the City School District by providing observations to aid in Committee on Special Education (CSE) sessions by providing clarification and support for services needed.

Program Goals

The goals of the WEE/WIN Inner-city Voucher Program are twofold:

1. Historically, Mr. and Mrs. Wegman gave $3 million dollars in 1993 for 14 preschool WEE (Wegman Early Childhood Education) programs. This included tuition aid to fami-lies, capital improvements to buildings and equipment. The main focus was to give inner-city youth the opportu-nity for a quality Catholic education. This program meets the needs of the inner-city child by providing a preschool, three- and four-year-old programs, as well as a before- and after-school care program.

2. In 1995, Mr. and Mrs. Wegman gave an additional $25 million dollars to stabilize enrollment in six inner-city

schools by making available monies to families for financial aid to supplement tuition. The program is called WIN (Wegman Inner-City Voucher Program).

Program Activities

The program operates educationally like other schools in the diocese. The schools' philosophies and mission are based on Gospel values, teaching Catholic doctrine and dogma with a strong emphasis on inclusivity, reflected in a spirit of ecumenism and evangelization. The challenge is to tend to academics needs while attending to the basic needs of food, clothing and shelter and nurturing a sense of self-worth and pride in the children. The six principals collaborate by meeting regularly to provide consistency in programming, services and grant funding. The assistant superintendent facilitates these meetings.

The tuition schedule and percentage of financial aid available is constant. Budget planning is processed through the assistant superintendent for the WIN programs and the assistant superintendent of finance along with the six principals.

Program Implementation

1. A strong commitment to Catholic schools, especially in the inner city, needs to be made by any diocese wishing to start a program similar to the WIN program. This firm commitment is what appealed to the Wegmans and helped them to make the tremendous pledge of assistance that continues to keep the six inner-city schools and their programs alive.

2. The key to the WIN schools' success is the coordination of resources by an assistant superintendent whose responsibilities are limited to the six schools. Moreover, the cooperation of the building principals is crucial, because the operating method is collaborative.

3. Inservicing teachers and staff is done collaboratively, resulting in more efficient use of time and resources.

4. Involvement of the community can result in partnerships between public agencies and the schools and the solicitation of an effective corps of volunteers.

Turner/Carroll PEP/LEEP Program—Providing Support to Low Performing Schools Fostering Greater Student Achievement

Turner/Carroll High School, Buffalo, New York

Program Description

To grow and provide quality education into the 21st century, Turner/Carroll is currently undergoing several transformations relating to type and number of youth it serves, sources of financial support and the type of education it will offer to students. Turner/Carroll has advanced from its humble beginning as a merger of two independent schools suffering from low enrollment and financial instability. For example, since the early 1980s, the student population of the school has changed from all White, Catholic to 97% African American, 1% Hispanic and other minorities who are non-Catholic, while enrollment has almost doubled from 1994 to 1997. During the next five years, Turner/Carroll will 1) become financially independent of the Diocese of Buffalo, 2) complete the process to obtain Middle Atlantic States Certification for the first time in its history and 3) transform into a college preparatory academy for socio-economically disadvantaged inner-city minority students.

However, the mission of Turner/Carroll High School remains the same—to provide an environment in which students are encouraged toward high academic achievement, a lifelong interest in learning, a positive self-image and an appreciation for cultural diversity so that they become responsible and productive citizens.

Over the last four years, the administration and staff have revitalized the spirit and focus of the school, vigorously marketed its academic programming and are collaborating with other educational institutions, such as the University of Buffalo, Niagara University, Canisius College and Hilbert College, for the first time for the benefit of the students. Turner/Carroll High School is also the only private high school in New York State to be a recipient of a NYNEX advanced teleconferencing and distance learning center as part of Buffalo CityNet.

Program Goals

The goals of the PEP/LEEP are to:

1. assess student competence levels,
2. identify and begin to develop strategies that will over- come any deficits,
3. facilitate a student enrichment program that extends the academic day and year,
4. increase student awareness of the value of a good educa- tion, and
5. instill in students that they will be held accountable for accomplishing academic achievement.

Program Activities

The Program is a collaborative venture orchestrating the day- to-day functions of a remedial/tutorial/enrichment program. Building on the strengths of the Broadway-Fillmore Neighborhood Initiative, which was formed as a problem-solv- ing police initiative embracing the ideologies of community policing, a community (neighborhood) initiative was developed. At its inception, the initiative was based on strengthening the following areas: 1) increased police visibility, 2) increased coor- dination between Precinct #11 with community and other com- munity agencies, 3) increased intern involvement and 4) reduced area crime. Neighborhood Initiatives utilized the Buffalo Police Department, Precinct #11, the criminal justice and human service department of Hilbert College.

Hilbert College students assist officers in staffing the remedial/tutorial/enrichment programs during summer and after-school sessions. The strategy is a comprehensive program aimed at reducing students' amount of free, unsupervised time. The completion of this clinical experience affords the interns course credit.

Turner/Carroll provides Project Enrichment, a strategic academic improvement plan comprised of a "Dream Team" of education- al consultants from University of Buffalo, State University College at Buffalo, Canisius College, Niagara University and Hilbert College. Students are encouraged to participate in a six- week summer and after school program that encourages academic success, a lifelong interest in learning that fosters a positive self image and an appreciation for cultural diversity. The experience encourages responsible and productive learning.

Turner/Carroll High School restructured its Academic Improvement Plan, a Business/Marketing Plan and Development Plan. The strategy was to foster academic success and reintroduce Christian values. A Homework Hotline, Homework Help Center, Chess Playing/Kite Flying Math Class and Club, A Future Business Leaders' Club, an after school Athletes' Tutorial Assistance Program, a Gemini Dance "flex and movement" physical education program, an annual Black History Play and Distance Learning Program were established as support and follow-up during the regular academic year.

Program Implementation

The backbone of PEP/LEEP is made strong by the dedication of the Hilbert College–Turner/Carroll educational connection, which may be helpful in replicating this program. The strong cooperation within the staff could provide other staff with the tools and instructional skills needed to adjust and tailor a program to fit particular school district needs. Mentoring would be provided on a scheduled basis and available to all interested in participating. In the instances where onsite personnel are identified, workshops would provide expertise to effectuate the following daily instructional activities in a similar PEP summer program.

9:00–11:30 a.m. — structured academic educational activities for the reluctant learner

12:00–1:00 p.m. — lunch provided with supervised staff

1:00–3:00 p.m. — recreational and craft activities for learners at low-performing levels

The workshop is proposed for teachers, staff and interns hoping to implement the program at a future time. It would be a weeklong inservice session 8:00 a.m.–3:00 p.m. Program planners believe that starting small and doing an excellent job will greatly improve results. A successful program attracts successful funding. Therefore, 50 to 100 youth would be a manageable target group.

Campaigns For Elementary School Endowments

Diocese of Toledo, Toledo, Ohio

Program Description

The Diocese of Toledo serves over 23,000 students in 87 elementary and 14 high schools. Over a third of the schools are more than a century old. Every type of school setting is represented: rural, small town, suburban, urban, inner-city. Student body sizes in the elementary schools range from 66 to 776 students.

In the mid-eighties the bishop and the superintendent of schools urged pastors and principals to establish an endowment fund for each school. They encouraged a goal of $1,000,000 per school by the year 2000. The superintendent visited each pastor to explain and encourage this plan.

The school office had a lawyer draw up a sample endowment charter which included these advantages:

- the pastor appointed the endowment trustees;
- the trustees decided if the investments were made locally or through the Catholic Foundation of the diocese;
- major donors received a copy of the charter and the bishop's written permission was required to invade the fund's principle (these items were safeguards);
- the charter stated where the endowment money would go, in case of the school's closure.

Furthermore, the school office assisted by:

- processing each school's application to establish its endowment,
- providing a part-time person who gave assistance (until 1991),
- collecting annual data on the endowment growth and reporting overall results to pastors and principals.

Gradually, 77 of the 87 elementary schools established endowments. Most school leaders did not know how to make the endowment grow. The charter did not name anyone responsible for securing gifts to the endowment. They had the tools but lacked the fund-raising know-how.

In October 1994, the schools office hired a full-time person, Sister Mary Burke. Her role is to increase the endowments in the schools. As the development consultant, she has two main responsibilities: 1) directing capital campaigns and 2) educating leaders about development.

Program Goals

Because each campaign takes approximately one year to complete, the development consultant works simultaneously with three separate campaigns, directing each campaign through all the phases.

1. Each of three campaigns will fund growth in the school endowment, but the campaigns also may include other parish and/or school purposes.

2. The main goal of every capital campaign is to secure the cash gifts which will fund the elementary school endowment (and other campaign purposes) and to secure planned gifts which will continue to finance the parish and the school in the future.

3. Another goal of the capital campaign is to teach local leaders the skills and attitudes necessary for success, thereby empowering them for similar efforts in the future.

4. The last goal is to let the example of success in one place encourage leaders in other schools to implement a similar effort.

Program Activities

The first phase of the campaign involves extensive consultation through a series of dinner meetings. Typically, 100-180 parishioners participate in this "mini-strategic planning process." At the end of the series of dinners, the leaders know:

1. whether parishioners want a capital campaign,

2. what growth in the school should be funded by the endowment interest and

3. what else in the parish and/or school, if anything, the campaign should include.

The second phase of the campaign invites the investment. Starting with pace-setting gifts, moving to leadership level gifts and then coming to the full parish for support, the campaign asks everyone to consider a "gift now"—a cash commitment over five years, and a "gift later"—a planned gift.

In the quiet phase of the campaign, leaders solicit major gifts in personal visits. They show the campaign video during these visits. After the advanced calls are completed, the leaders determine the dollar goal of the campaign. Then the campaign is presented to the full parish in several steps, with steps 2 through 6 compressed into two weeks. These steps are:

1. campaign orientation meeting for leaders of every parish group,
2. campaign orientation meeting for active parishioners (those who belong to parish organizations),
3. campaign meeting for parents of current students in the school,
4. presentation at all Masses at which parishioners receive campaign literature and pledge forms,
5. phonathon to remind people to bring pledge forms on Commitment Weekend, and
6. phonathon to those who did not pledge.

Program Implementation
Initially
- Meet with pastor and principal.
- Meet with parish leaders to explain campaign, ask reactions.

Phase One: Building the Bedrock (3-4 months)
- Establish a Steering Committee to oversee consultation process.
- Conduct dinner meetings with 100-180 parishioners (total) to identify hopes, dreams and to ask their opinions about the campaign.
- Phone key people who did not attend the dinner for mini-interview.
- Determine campaign purposes based on consultation.

Work of the Steering Committee is now completed.

Phase Two: Inviting the Investment (9-12 months)

Quiet Phase (1-2 months)

- Prepare and complete video script, filming, editing.
- Set up a selection and enlistment task force to identify chair and members of the executive committee based on criteria provided.
- Have pastor recruit chair and executive committee members in person.
- Recruit a planned giving committee to help as needed throughout this phase.

Quiet Phase continues with executive committee in charge of campaign (2-5 months)

- Identify major donors, rate prospects, train solicitors for personal visits with potential major donors (3-5 months).
- Conduct visits for major gifts, use video case statement in calls, bring planned giving specialist, if appropriate.
- Report progress every two weeks, assign more calls, recruit and train new solicitors to make calls at the next levels.
- Print campaign literature and be ready to distribute.

Public Phase launched (1 month)

- Invite leaders of all parish organizations to campaign meeting, ask their assistance, secure their pledge commitments.
- Conduct large group meetings for active parishioners.
- Present campaign at meeting for parents of school children.
- Have pastor speak at all the Masses one weekend, campaign packets distributed after Masses.
- Remind people via phonathon to return pledges on Commitment Weekend.
- Bring pledges to altar during offertory on Commitment Weekend.
- Phone those who did not return pledge forms.
- Structure some planned giving educational and promotional opportunities.

Executive committee has completed its role. Billing, acknowl-
edging, reporting to the parish becomes the parish office staff
responsibility.

Fundraising Programs at St. Philip the Apostle School

St. Philip the Apostle School, Pasadena, California

Program Description

There are six financial programs at St. Philip the Apostle School:
Tuition Plan that includes tuition assistance, *Scrip Program*,
*Annual Giving Campaign Program, Parent Teacher Organization
Fundraising Program,* the *Endowment Program* and the *Grant
Program.* Each entity administers its own programs, which are
coordinated with the school principal to ensure that the neces-
sary operating and project funds of the school are available.

The *Tuition Plan*, coupled with service hours, provides the
school with the necessary day-to-day operating funds and additional assistance required for successful operation of the school.

The *Scrip Program* requires that each family purchase $2,500 in
scrip for the year.

The *Annual Giving Campaign* is a yearly solicitation of parents,
parishioners, alumni, grandparents, school board, faculty, staff,
and businesses. The campaign has an annual goal of $100,000
of unrestricted funds for the school's operating budget.

The *Parent Teacher Organization Fundraising Program (PTO)*
has a board of its own and has provided the school with over
$65,000 as of June 1997. The PTO oversees a number of money-
raising and community-building activities, including the Fall
Festival, and the Spring Dinner Dance and Auction.

The *Endowment Program* maintains a pool of restricted assets,
designated to be held in perpetuity.

The *Grants Program* identifies funding sources for specific
needs as designated by the principal.

These programs ensure the quality of Catholic education
offered at St. Philip for all students, provide affordable tuition
for all parish and community families, and maintain financial

stability for the school. In 1991-92, St. Philip the Apostle School had 350 students (327 parishioners and 23 non-parishioners). Today the school enrolls 419 students (359 Catholics, 294 families of whom 223 are parishioners).

Program Goals

The *Tuition Plan* consists of four service/volunteer plans available depending upon the number of children in the family attending the school, parishioner status and the parents' ability to complete service/volunteer hours. A tuition coordinator is on staff to assist families with their financial obligations. The net-to-bad-debt ratio is less than 1/2 of 1% of an annual tuition income of $750,000. Giving families a choice enables St. Philip to provide a Catholic education for all economic levels within our parish and community.

The *Scrip Program* requires that each family purchase $2,500 in scrip ($1,500 for single parent families) spread out over the ten-month school year. Scrip is redeemable for groceries, clothing, etc. at grocery and department stores within the area. The school receives 4% of all scrip sold, and last year raised a total of $32,000 from the Scrip Program.

The *Annual Giving Campaign,* "Blessed Are The Children" is a yearly solicitation of parents, parishioners, alumni, grandparents, school board, faculty, staff, and local businesses with an annual goal of $100,000. This money is unrestricted income and supports the general operating budget of the school. Donors have the option of making a pledge, which can be fulfilled in monthly installments, payable in full by the end of the school year. Faculty and staff have the opportunity for direct payroll deductions to be made monthly.

The *Parent Teacher Organization Fundraising Program* oversees a number of fundraising and community-building activities during the school year, including the annual Fall Fest, and the spring Dinner Dance and Auction. In addition, the Boosters Club raises funds for the after-school sports program. The Booster Club is considered a committee within the PTO and operates with its own committee members.

The *Endowment Program* solicits gifts once a year for the Endowment Fund. In 1997, members of the parish were invited by the pastor to attend a luncheon hosted by a founding board member. Two current students and one graduate spoke on the value of the education they received at St. Philip. A total of $134,000 was raised at the luncheon, bringing the total of the endowment fund to over $200,000. Parishioners and parents make memorial and tribute gifts to the fund throughout the year.

The *Grants Program* in the 1996–97 school year was very successful in receiving over $40,000 of restricted gifts for plan improvement, classroom materials, staff compensation and staff development. The Grant Ad Hoc Committee under the direction of the development director attempts to write at least three grant proposals every year.

Program Activities

1. The *Annual Giving Campaign*: Blessed Are the Children

There are seven phases or groups included in the solicitation of funds for the annual campaign, each with an individual goal as follows: Parents, $37,000; Parishioners, $35,000; School board, $20,000; Faculty/Staff, $1,500; Grandparents, $3,000; Alumni, $2,500 and Business, $1,000.

Solicitation begins in September, with the deadline for pledges to be paid in full by June 30 of the school year. The campaign is the responsibility of the development director and the annual campaign committee of the school board.

The Parent Phase of the campaign begins in September. Packets explaining the annual campaign are sent home to parents in the weekly family envelope. Approximately two weeks later, a phonathon is held and parents who have not made a pledge are contacted. Should a family find the monetary gift to be a hardship, a Gift of Prayer is an alternative. Status updates of the campaign are furnished to parents via a newsletter prepared by the development director and sent to each family monthly.

The Parish Phase follows the mailing of the annual report and is completed before November 1. Every parishioner receives a letter, signed by the pastor, with a pledge envelope. The Sunday bulletin furnishes updates on the progress of this phase and no solicitation of funds is made from November 1 through

Easter Sunday when the parish is involved is special collections determined by the Archdiocese.

A faculty chair and the development director coordinate the Faculty/Staff Phase. Each person makes a monetary or prayer pledge; cash pledges may be directly deducted from the monthly paycheck.

The alumni chair and a sub-committee of four to six alumni coordinate the Alumni Phase. A solicitation letter is sent with a personal note to graduates, including those who graduated as far back as the 1940s. In conjunction with this, an Alumni Homecoming is held every three years to welcome back former students at a special Mass, reception and tour of the school.

The Business Phase includes solicitation of local businesses, matching grants from employers of parents and parishioners and designated gifts through United Way.

2. The *Parent Teacher Organization Fundraising Program* (PTO)
The two major fundraisers for the 1996–97 school year were the Fall Festival and the Dinner Dance/Auction. Net profit from the Fall Festival was in excess of $39,000, and from the Dinner Dance/Auction, $33,000.

3. The *Endowment Program*
An endowment is a pool of assets, restricted and designated to be held in perpetuity. Only the income from these funds is used for operations or special projects. The endowment program was established in 1989 to address the ongoing need for tuition assistance among the poor families of St. Philip the Apostle parish and to maintain ongoing capital expenditures.

The *Endowment Fund* was founded with a $50,000 gift from an Endowment Campaign. It is part of the school's overall long-range plan, and is managed within the overall context of development efforts.

4. The *Grants Program*
The development director and the Grants Ad Hoc Committee collaborate to research funding sources for the specific needs of the school as determined by the principal. Grant monies are received by writing and responding to grant proposals from foundations and organizations and some government entities.

Program Implementation

1. The *Tuition Plan, Scrip Program, Annual Giving Campaign, Parent Teacher Organization Fundraising Program, Endowment Program* and the *Grants Program* can only be as successful as the pastor, principal and parents/teachers desire them to be. The pastor must be a firm believer in Catholic education. The principal must be both practical and visionary. The parents must want more than just an education for their children; they must want to be involved in that educational process. Teachers and staff must be committed to the students in their charge.

2. Excellence in education is not dependent upon great sums of money, but rather on how that money is utilized. The school is a business and must be operated as such. Sound financial practices must be employed.

3. A vision for the future must be desired. Contentment with the status quo cannot be tolerated if the school is to become successful both academically and financially. Growth in all financial programs should be ongoing.

4. All schools regardless of their setting or status can adapt these practices and programs to their individual schools. Education of parents and parishioners in the program enable them to understand their financial responsibility.

5. Parents, pastors and educators should meet and decide what is important to the school. Collaboration with other schools who have similar programs in effect can be helpful.

Child Care and Parenting Skills Program

Nazareth Regional High School, Brooklyn, New York

Program Description

Nazareth Regional High School offers a two-part, one-semester elective in child care to juniors and seniors. The course offers an opportunity to non-college bound students, thus attracting these students to enroll in the school, and provides non-tuition income to the school through the leasing of the child care and pre-school operation.

Program Goals

The objectives of Nazareth Regional High School's Child Care and Parenting Skills program are multiple:

1. to realize income from unused space in the building,
2. to attract and retain students whose goals do not include college,
3. to provide direct instruction for students in all areas of child care, and
4. to provide additional income to teachers and staff members employed by the school.

Program Activities

Nazareth offers a two-part one-semester elective, open to juniors and seniors, titled Child Care I and Child Care II.

These students are enrolled in a program which includes 40 hours of classroom instruction, 15 hours of service carried out at the Preschool Center for Handicapped Children which is located in our building, and appropriate field visitations (to a local college's own clinical preschool operation, for instance).

The service in the preschool center is carried out under the supervision of the Nazareth faculty member assigned to this project as well as by the preschool's teaching staff. It emphasizes observation, reflection and hands-on activities.

Field visits provide an enriching perspective, usually provided by St. Joseph's College's Dillon Center, which funds this project.

Program Implementation

The program is easily adaptable in inner-city schools, large and small, by virtue of the following characteristics often associated with this type of school:

- extra space,
- the need to develop non-tuition sources of revenue,
- large proportion of single-parent families,
- large proportion of households in which child-care is a need, regardless of the number of parents on hand, and
- disproportionately high incidence of adolescent pregnancy.

While the school is less confident in addressing the issues of rural and/or multi-grade classrooms, it believes its program addresses needs on issues so central to the mission of the Catholic school that its relevance would emerge, whatever the setting.

Fill Every Desk

Dayton Catholic Elementary School, Dayton, Ohio

Program Description

In a neighborhood where Catholic school tuition and Catholic school costs were becoming out of reach, Dayton Catholic Elementary School was faced in 1995 with a declining enrollment and the possibility of closure. The incoming president of Key Corps suggested that, by increasing enrollment, the per pupil costs would decrease. Bolstered by state monies allotted through two programs of mandated services reimbursement, the principal and the staff realized that, even if additional students paid no tuition, the per pupil reimbursement from the State of Ohio would provide income over and above tuition monies. Using the Tuition Aid Date Services program recommended by the archdiocese, the school could determine the amount of tuition that interested parents could afford. With a minimum expected tuition of $12.50 per week, the school embarked on a recruitment program for additional students.

Program Goals

The Goals of the program are:

1. to fill what would have been empty desks with a student paying less than the original set tuition, if the family qualified for aid, keeping in mind that the student generated $350 in state revenues over and above the tuition for the school,
2. to reduce the cost per pupil to lower than the stated tuition, and
3. to demonstrate the desire of families for a Catholic value-based education and provide a giving opportunity for like-minded benefactors.

Program Activities

The first order of business was to enlist the teaching staff as primary recruiters and enthusiastic supporters of what is now called the "Fill Every Desk" campaign. The teachers would also become the initial contact between the parent and the school. As parents called in, their names and phone numbers would be given to the grade-level teacher who would be instructing their children.

Meetings were held with parents, area civic leaders and ministers in surrounding churches to enlist their help in recruiting families who wanted a Christian value-based education for their children.

Teachers called, and continue to call, all interested parents, inviting them to the school, answering questions regarding what the school could do for their children and often helping parents fill out registration and tuition aid forms. They repeatedly told parents that money should not be a deterrent since tuition aid was available.

Very soon after each tuition aid report was delivered to the school, the principal contacted each family and negotiated a tuition which the family could afford. Teachers then began telling their stories to potential benefactors in order to gather the tuition assistance necessary to meet the needs of the families. The Archbishop of Cincinnati led the way in recognizing the value of Catholic schools in urban areas. His annual $100,000-plus contribution became tuition assistance when the 218th student enrolled. With the archbishop's contributions, teachers were able to gather over $800,000 for family need for a three-year pilot project. Several area Catholic churches have pledged and/or contributed nearly $100,000 for this campaign.

Within six weeks, the student population grew from the original 97 students to 218 on July 15. This number was significant because the cost of educating a student literally dropped from $5,000 to $2,250, which was the tuition charged for the 1995–96 school year.

The school is very clear in its philosophy statement that children will not be denied entrance based on economic factors. For the first time, the school is truly accessible to all families, regardless of financial resources.

Program Implementation

Since those initial beginnings in June 1995, the teachers of Dayton Catholic have engaged four other Dayton Catholic urban schools and schools from Wapakoneta and Greenville in Ohio and, most recently, a school in Covington, Kentucky, in the Fill Every Desk campaign. All of the schools which have heard the stories and implemented the program have witnessed dramatic increases in enrollment.

The important staff development aspect of this project is the teacher-to-teacher training provided by the staff of Dayton Catholic. By explaining the simple features of teacher and parent contact early in the recruitment process of new students, other teachers see the value of establishing this important relationship.

Dayton Catholic already has provided staff development in the "Fill Every Desk" model. The staff is exploring the opportunity to work with the local university to teleconference with interested schools.

The BISON Fund *(Buffalo Inner-City Scholarship Opportunity Network)*

Buffalo, New York

Program Description

The BISON Fund is a privately funded, tax-exempt foundation classified as a 501(c)(3) organization under the Internal Revenue Code of 1954. The foundation is supported by voluntary tax-deductible contributions from individuals, foundations and corporations. No donations are used for administrative costs of salaries or overhead. Every dollar raised goes toward a scholarship for a deserving family. Administrative costs are raised separately through grants and private donations. The number of scholarships is limited by the amount of money raised by the BISON Fund.

Students fill out applications to be considered for the scholarships. To be eligible for a scholarship the child must:

1. live in the Buffalo public school district,
2. be entering grades K-8,

3. qualify for the federal free or reduced school lunch program, and

4. have met all admission requirements at the accredited school he/she desires to attend.

Applicants who meet all four criteria are randomly selected and awarded scholarships on the first come, first served basis. It is not an academic scholarship but a need-based scholarship. The only academic requirement is that the student continues to have passing grades. Scholarships are awarded for a minimum of three years. BISON will contribute 50% of the tuition cost of any private school in the Buffalo area up to a maximum of $700, payable directly to the school. (Note: the average annual tuition of private grammar schools in the city of Buffalo is approximately $1,400.)

Program Goals

The overall goal is to provide children with better educational opportunities.

BISON awards scholarships to give as many low-income families as possible the ability to choose a private or parochial school for their children despite their financial situation. Most of the students go to local private and parochial schools because they feel the smaller classrooms, individual attention and discipline create a more positive learning environment. (Note: the BISON Fund also supports students' decisions to attend other private, non-Catholic schools.)

Program Activities

The BISON Fund engages in the following activities:

1. Establishes, organizes and manages the business and administrative affairs of the foundation, including all basic and standard components such as telephones, office facilities, business equipment and support services.

2. Carries out all policies and achieves the goals set by the foundation's board of directors (trustees).

3. Develops and maintains a database of schools, students, mailing lists, donors and potential donors.

4. Performs all tasks necessary for the establishment and the efficient running of the program, including school and

parent/student correspondence, student monitoring and scholarship payments.

5. Reports to the board of directors on budgetary matters relating to all aspects of the program including administrative and scholarship funds.

6. Works with the board on all matters relating to program design and interpretation and the dissemination of public information.

7. Develops and issues operating reports with respect to the program, as required by the board, but not less than monthly.

Program Implementation

1. Identify potential donors.
2. Gather information on other scholarship efforts.
3. Identify local educational situation and need.
4. Contact potential donors.
5. Identify beneficiary group.
6. Conduct a confidential survey of public and private schools.
7. Develop proposed scholarship amount.
8. Develop preliminary program design.
9. Design application process.
10. Create a timeline for start-up.
11. Identity administrative needs.
12. Establish the legal entity.
13. Identity data processing requirements.
14. Identity in-kind contribution requirements.

Chapter 3

A Plan to Pay for Catholic Schools

– Joseph Claude Harris

1. We Need a New Plan

The present method of finding the cash to pay Catholic school bills contributes to a situation where schools enroll diminishing proportions of the Catholic student population. Andrew Greeley described this evolution in a 1989 *America* article. Greeley wrote, "Catholic schools seem to be entering a twilight, not facing immediate extinction, perhaps, but slipping slowly into darkness."[1] The current Catholic school funding model can best be described by eavesdropping on the regular December school commission meeting for St. Sample parish in Somewheresville, USA. The task of constructing a budget for the subsequent school year usually starts when the commission chair quizzes the head of the parent's club: "How much money can you raise next year?" The answer to that question leads to a second inquiry asked of the group at large: "How much subsidy can we hope for from the parish?"

Such informal survey results provide the basis for designing the elastic element of the budget process, next year's tuition schedule. Should subsidy be static or perhaps even shrinking and fundraising should be stagnant, then parents must fund teacher salary increases or new science textbooks by increasing tuition rates. The problem with the present system is that it works well when parents can afford to pick up the tab; otherwise, schools simply close. Some of each has been happening over the past 30 years.

Data describing enrollment and funding patterns illustrate the evolution of Catholic school structures since the early sixties. Catholic schools registered about 47 percent of a Catholic school-age population of 11.447 million in 1962.[2] When the National Catholic Educational Association first surveyed elementary school finances, parishes paid 63 percent of elementary school costs in 1969.[3] In the three decades since Neuwien's estimate of participation, the proportion of Catholics enrolled in schools plummeted to 18 percent of a school-age population of 11.754 million for 1991.[4] Similar change affected parish support. Subsidy paid for 25 percent of elementary school costs for 1994.[5] Clearly, Catholic schools have evolved from a church-funded endeavor managed by professed religious to a system of largely parent-funded programs for a diminishing portion of the registered Catholic school population.

Since tuition charges limit educational opportunity, Catholic school managers need to consider a plan that can lead to a different destination than the present direction of gradual evolution to a system of schools completely supported by parents paying for the costs of the programs that survive. School costs have grown dramatically. For example, parish elementary school budgets ballooned by an average annual rate of 9.4 percent between 1980 and 1989.[6] School costs grew at twice the rate of inflation for the decade of the eighties.[7] School leaders coped with much larger school expenses by increasing tuition at an average annual rate of 12.4 percent.[8] The current economic model of Catholic school funding points inevitably in the direction of declining market share. Fewer Catholics will be able in the future to afford a program where user fees grow at triple the rate of inflation.

A planning model defined by Peter Drucker in a 1994 *Harvard Business Review* article can be used to develop a theory of business for Catholic schools. In speaking of circumstances that need a new plan for doing business, Drucker described a situation that many Catholic school administrators will recognize.

> *The story is a familiar one: a company that was a super-star only yesterday finds itself stagnating and frustrated, in trouble, and often in a seemingly unmanageable crisis. This phenomenon is no means confined to the United States...Also, it occurs just as often outside businesses—in labor unions, government agencies, hospitals, museums, and churches. In fact, it seems even less tractable in those areas.*[9]

Drucker goes on to explain that the cause of the crises affecting such commercial behemoths as IBM is not that things are being done poorly. IBM flourished in a time when producing hardware held the key to success in the information processing industry. IBM managers never really relinquished the vision of software as an adjunct to making machines. Bill Gates and Steve Baumer at Microsoft saw the future of economically priced software and the rest is history. Probably the best illustration of how poorly IBMers understood the software revolution can be found in the installation instructions for Microsoft's Windows and IBM's competitor product, OS/2. The Microsoft system required that the customer only know how to type "install;" the IBM product came with a very unfriendly 114-page installation manual.

In the case of Catholic schools, commentators regularly laud the success of these programs even in desperate urban circumstances where public education sometimes fails to produce a preponderance of literate graduates. The problem is that the assumptions on which the organization has been built no longer fit reality. At one time, elementary schools were a relatively low-cost parish program paid for by the pastor from the proceeds of the Sunday collection. Secondary schools often flourished as the apostolates of teaching women and men religious. Parents now pay for two-thirds of elementary school costs that total as much as the entire revenue of the sponsoring parish. Alums and parents furnish over 90 percent of the program cost for largely lay-staffed secondary schools. Over the past three decades the funding model for Catholic education has undergone a revolution. Drucker's approach of analyzing organizational environment, mission and competencies can be used profitably to develop a new economic model for Catholic schools, one that deals with the radically different facts affecting the present management of schools.

2. A Theory of Business

Catholic education does seem to need a different way of thinking. Let's face it. The past 35 years have represented an upheaval for Catholic school programs. The net number of schools has dropped from 13,208 in 1961 to 8,250 for 1996. Enrollment declined from 5.462 million to 2.55 million for the same time period. The Catholic school-age population grew from 11.447 million in 1961 to 11.754 million for 1991. The present school model works for those who can afford tuition payments. The dilemma lies in the fact that the number of participants continues to shrink as a proportion of the potential population. These data suggest a need for a new method of organizing programs.

Any Catholic school administrator looking to learn about business thinking would immediately be confronted by a myriad of new management techniques: downsizing, out-sourcing, total quality management, economic value analysis, reengineering, etc. Picture yourself as a school superintendent standing in front of a rack of shelves in a bookstore, wondering which volume contains secrets that address present management difficulties confronting Catholic educators. You may be tempted to close your eyes and grab. Such a random approach to selecting a business theory would likely miss the mark. Much of what presently occupies bookstore shelves describes how to do differently what is already being done. Yet, doing Catholic education differently would make little sense given that researchers and commentators consistently praise Catholic programs as models of success. Rather, the challenge facing Catholic educational managers lies more in the realm of developing a business theory that leads to more effective revenue strategies than endlessly increasing tuition. Catholic leaders need to examine the organizational structure of Catholic education rather than the classroom content.

Peter Drucker outlined an approach to developing a business theory suited to the present situation of Catholic education. Drucker stressed that "what to do" is increasingly the central challenge facing managements, especially those of big companies that have enjoyed long-term success.[10] The cause of the crises affecting such giants as IBM and General Motors is not that things are being done poorly. It is not even that the wrong things are being done. The problem is that the assumptions on which the organization has been built and is being run no longer fit reality.

Drucker sees three groups of assumptions shaping any organization's behavior. First, managers must make assumptions about the nature of the world they live in. They must discern the shape of society and various markets with that social structure. They need to define and locate customers and understand how technology shapes customer expectations. After studying their culture, managers must define concretely their mission within that broader culture. Hoping to do good and avoid evil does not count as a mission statement. Rather, managers must specify concretely what it is they intend to accomplish, for whom, and at what cost. Finally, modern managers must work to secure the key skills and resources necessary to accomplish their mission. Aspiring to walk on the moon makes no sense unless one starts to build a rocket. The combination of these assumptions is what a company gets paid for and represents that company's theory of business.

Catholic schools presently operate in somewhat the same fashion as IBM, successful yet struggling. Bishops and priests originally built Catholic schools to preserve the faith of poor immigrants. Realizing their flock flooded through Ellis Island with only the possessions they could carry, church leaders operated schools substituting the contributed services of women and men religious for access to public tax revenue. Not needing public dollars gave Catholic school leaders the option of ignoring public educational philosophy and practices. Pastors and principals prided themselves on running programs free from the Protestant world of public education.

To put it mildly, this world has changed. Vatican II happened and, as the late Archbishop Connolly of Seattle once put it, "no one does what they are told anymore." In addition, contributed services fell by the wayside, a victim of the actuarial reality of lengthened life spans for religious and the dwindling membership of groups of professed sisters and brothers. Retired sisters, brothers and priests now often require expensive medical care, a situation not anticipated in the fiscal design of religious communities. The total number of sisters has dropped from about 180,000 in the heyday of the construction of large convents adjacent to equally large schools to the present membership of somewhat less than 100,000. Finally, Catholic laity themselves have journeyed over the years from the initial situation of poor, urban immigrants to the modestly affluent category of suburban Americans. For today's Catholic, the need to spend millions on buildings and programs intended to preserve an immigrant faith seems less obvious.

Drucker suggests a three-step process for the development of a business theory. He recommends starting any planning process with an analysis of the present state of the industry. Who are the customers, what are the costs, and where are the competitors? The second step involves the development of specific mission statements. Finally, the planning process ends with a listing of specific strategies needed to accomplish the agreed-upon mission of the organization. The effective use of planning requires a conviction that no present practice is sacred. Educational planning can be of no use if Catholic educators insist that current classroom successes constitute the core mission of Catholic education. Such satisfaction with current programs would perpetuate the present evolution to a tuition-supported system educating a dwindling portion of the Catholic population. If, on the other hand, Catholic leaders intend to manage the future of Catholic schools, then the business theory process developed by Drucker offers a useful approach to solving current organizational problems.

The first step in a planning process designed to address the "what to do" question involves a study of the present state of the educational industry in the United States. For Catholic leaders, such an approach represents a distinct departure from past practice. Catholics originally started schools because they wanted no part of the King James Version of the bible common in public programs in the late nineteenth century. For the present, though, it is critical for Catholic leaders to realize that they are influenced by problems and parental expectations affecting the entire educational industry. Catholic elementary principals currently stress the development of computer labs because such programs are both needed and expected. Catholic lay faculties often peg salary expectations to at least a proportion of public school scale. In our planning discussion, we will look first at public perceptions and funding problems confronting public education. The insights gained from this investigation should guide a subsequent development of ideas about the mission of Catholic education and the strategies required to accomplish this mission.

3. Problems Plaguing Public Education

Public school funding headaches exist at every level. Two related problems have contributed to an unfortunate situation where some public school districts cannot pay anticipated bills. First, survey results show shaky support for public education programs. School leaders simply do not operate schools that meet customer expectations. A second problem related to parent frustration comes from a clash in funding expectations. Educators talk of implementing computer-based program enhancements requiring more money, while economic evidence suggests Americans do not want to spend much beyond the cost of inflation to increase funding for present education programs.

A. What Do Parents Want?

The answer may be: It depends on whom you talk to. Opinion research strongly suggests that significant portions of the population hold divergent views about the condition of public education programs. The situation resembles the Irish definitions for an optimist and a pessimist. An optimist sees a partly-filled glass of whiskey as half-full while a pessimist views the same portion of alcohol as half-empty. One national research project and two reports recently described in the Seattle media all show similar results. Americans don't agree about the effectiveness of public education programs.

A recent survey cosponsored by the New York-based Public Agenda and the Institute for Educational Leadership in Washington, DC, reported that, "over half (55%) of the public and 71 percent of parents with children currently attending public school initially give schools in their community a 'good' or 'excellent' rating."[11] These expressions of satisfaction coexist in a context where media articles chronicling declining test scores abound and some public officials either seek to sponsor radical changes in educational management or lament what they see as the present failure of the educational system.

Daniel Yankelovich offered a principle to evaluate puzzling positive answers in public opinion survey projects. One should always track consistency when costs and other specifics associated with a course of action are made clear. In other words, the devil is always in the details. It seems that many Americans respond positively to a general question about rating schools. This support weakens, however, when the audience considers concrete concerns. For example, 55 percent of respondents rated schools good or excellent. "This support disintegrated the moment the questionnaire turned to specifics: 72 percent voiced concern about drugs and violence in local schools, 61 percent said low standards were a problem, 60 percent complained about a lack of attention to basics."[12]

Public support for schools does mean something. Parents respect the local community and the teachers they know. This generally positive feeling, however, does mask many concerns that lie just beneath the surface of community sentiment. It would be a mistake for educational administrators to feel that a 55 percent positive rating indicates solid community support. Parents and the community worry about the present state of education programs.

The Public Agenda survey further tested the strength of support for public schools by asking respondents to compare public and private programs. The results were startling:

*Sixty-one percent of Americans surveyed say private
schools are more likely to provide order and discipline in
the classroom, compared to only 18 percent who say that
their local public schools do better. Fifty-three percent
say private schools have higher academic standards compared to 24 percent for public schools. Fifty-one percent
say private schools offer more safety and security to 20
percent for public schools. Over half say private schools
are better at providing an environment that promotes
values such as honesty and responsibility.[13]*

Certainly, the most ominous statistic of the entire project was
the finding that almost six in ten (57%) parents with children in
public schools would send their children to private schools if
they could afford to do so. The comparison to private education highlights what the public expects of educational programs—safety, order, emphasis on the basics and smaller classes. It is in looking for these values that the support for public
education falters.

Two opinion projects reported in the Seattle, WA, media
appear to show contradictory results. The *Seattle Times* presented one project with the headline, "Schools Make the
Grade."[14] The data from this project show positive results.
Thirty-eight percent of parents reported that they were very
satisfied with educational offerings while 39 percent gave an
evaluation of somewhat satisfied. Several days after the *Times*
description of happy school district customers, the *Post
Intelligencer* published a survey that chronicled the worries of
registered voters. Education was the top topic. These data
show that many Washingtonians feel that public education is
worse today than it was four years ago.[15] Twenty percent
strongly agree while 38 percent agree that educational quality
is worse. The results of the two surveys suggest the puzzling
conclusion that citizens are satisfied with a program that is
gradually deteriorating.

Two trends are consistent in both polls. A sizable group of parents (38%) are very satisfied while a large contingent of registered voters (29.1%) disagrees with the proposition that educational quality has worsened. The positives seem firm at about
35 percent. At the same time, a large group of parents (23%)
are dissatisfied with programs while a sizable chunk of voters

(19%) strongly agree that educational quality is going downhill. The negatives seem to be consistent at about 20 percent.

The real question comes in trying to handicap the attitudes of the group between strong positive and strong negative. One significant pattern does emerge from this middle group. Virtually every parent had an opinion when asked about satisfaction levels; 13 percent of voters—a much broader audience—had no opinion. We need to address, then, the meaning of somewhat satisfied (39%) in the poll of parents and agree (38.1%) that things are worsening in the research querying the worries of all registered voters. Perhaps somewhat satisfied and agree are not contradictory. The middle group might best be described as positive and worried and uneasy at the same time. Such an interpretation leaves us with a consistent picture of attitudes toward education of 35 percent positive, 35 percent uneasy and worried, 20 percent negative, and 10 percent with no opinion.

Given such fragmented support for public education, we should not be surprised to find that segments of the population both in Washington State and around the nation endorse experiments to accomplish the goal of safe, basic education for all students. The Public Agenda researchers found 28 percent favored an overhaul of public education while 28 percent supported tuition vouchers. Only 20 percent saw the solution as a business-as-usual approach of bolstering present efforts with more money. A surprisingly large group (10%) chose the radical approach of privatization where a company would be hired to run a school or group of schools. Other respondents were unsure or leaned toward state management of schools.

B. School Costs as a Proportion of American Resources

A second problem confronting educational leaders is a significant change in the share of resources provided education both in the United States and in Washington State over the past decade. In the United States we no longer give an increasing proportion of our funds to K-12 programs. The Gross Domestic Product represents the broadest measure of American resources. In 1984, Americans spent 4 percent or $149 billion of that year's GDP on K-12 programs. The proportion of the 1990 GDP of 5.55 trillion allocated to education increased to 4.5 percent or $249 billion. GDP for 1993 was 6.34 trillion. The American school budget for that year was approximately $295 billion or a constant 4.5 percent.[16] Americans stopped increasing the K-12 share of the nation's budget around 1990.

The fact that educational spending no longer grows as a share of resources has a dramatic impact on program funding. Per pupil cost increased by $280 annually between 1984 and 1990. The national increase in per pupil expenditures dropped to $184 per year between 1990 and 1993. The impact for inflation was similar for both periods. Inflation cost $131 annually between 1984 and 1990 and $144 per year for the more recent period. What changed was the amount available for program modification. Between 1984 and 1990 educators had $149 per student beyond the cost of inflation to spend each year on program enhancement. That number dropped to $40 per student per year since 1990.

A similar pattern occurred in Washington state. Per pupil cost increased by $275 annually between 1984 and 1990. The state annual increase in per pupil cost declined to $183 between 1990 and 1993. Inflation cost $136 annually between 1984 and 1990; the cost of inflation grew only slightly to $147 per year after 1990.[17] Funds available for program change dropped drastically between the two periods from $139 per student per year between 1984 and 1990 to just $36 per student in recent years. Both in the country and in Washington state, increased funds since 1990 have gone almost entirely to pay for growing enrollments and inflation. Little remains in the educational budget to pay for program modifications.

These budgetary constraints combine with a situation of unhappy or worried customers to provide a picture of an industry on the verge of significant innovation. It is likely that parents who do not want to purchase the present educational product will find alternative programs. The pattern of public per pupil costs growing at twice the rate of inflation has ended. Educators react negatively to cost-conscious legislators who push charter schools and voucher programs in response to demands from their constituents. The industry future, however, clearly belongs to educational programs willing to live with greatly changed circumstances.

4. How to Write a Mission Statement for Catholic Schools

The second step in the planning process outlined by Peter Drucker calls for the definition of a mission statement. Such a summary of purpose follows logically from a consideration of a particular industry environment. A mission statement represents a set of choices made after a consideration of all the facts. To better understand the process of making choices in the development of an educational plan, we will look first at the educational mission statement developed by Catholic bishops in 1884. What was the state of the culture and the education industry that caused these men to put their energies into the construction of schools? The process that they confirmed in their Baltimore meeting energized the American Catholic Church for about 80 years and resulted in the construction of over 13,000 elementary and secondary schools. Once we see how this mission statement gave formal approval to a schools movement in the last century, we can then summarize present educational circumstances and offer ideas about a mission statement that fit the situation of Catholic education in America.

The first colonists saw schools as the normal means for instilling loyalty to the sponsoring confessional group. Concern over any separation of church and state did not trouble these original Americans. The oldest piece of public legislation on schools is the famous "Old Deluder" Act of 1647, tightly linking the school and religious formation.[18] The Act referred to "ye ould deluder, Satan, who keepe men from the knowledge of ye Scriptures." The legislation thwarted the work of Satan by requiring each township of 50 households or more to appoint a teacher and set up a school.

Catholics generally lived on the periphery of the community during the colonial period. They were deprived of freedom to worship together, to take part in public life and to educate their children. By 1704, even Catholic-founded Maryland had passed "An Act to Prevent the Growth of Popery," among whose provisions was one which threatened to deport any Catholic who should keep school, board students or instruct children.[19]

After the Revolution, Protestant school leaders sought to develop a program that emphasized the common interests and beliefs of the various denominations. The movement for a common American school relied heavily on the leadership of Horace Mann who held the position of secretary to the Massachusetts Board of Education between 1837 and 1848. Mann's program called for a Christian religion that could transcend the distinctive beliefs of Congregationalist or Methodist or Episcopal or Baptist. The cornerstone of Mann's religion was the Bible, the great symbol and source of Protestant Christianity. Provided the public school did not favor any special church or sect, it remained free to teach the agreed moral and religious truths found in the common Bible.[20]

As a result of waves of immigration after 1850, large numbers of Catholics faced the dilemma of sending their children to a school system that threatened their beliefs. The public school of the time was not only Protestant-oriented but often belligerently so. The textbooks contained many derogatory references to Catholic beliefs and structures. The widely-used *New England Primer* with its warning: "Child, behold that Man of Sin, the Pope, worthy of thy utmost hatred," is simply one case.[21] The Protestant orientation of the public schools, though generally diminishing as the nineteenth century closed, was the principal reason that led the Catholic community to establish separate schools.[22]

Since the educational industry and the American culture were hostile to Catholics, small wonder that American bishops voted to affirm the establishment of a parish school system when they convened in Baltimore in 1884. The assembled bishops offered a mission statement that was specific and well understood by the membership of the American Catholic church. They directed that every church build a school, period. Any priest who did not fulfill this dictum deserved to be removed from his church. The bishop's mission statement defined a clear choice for American Catholics. Religious education was the program priority for the immigrant church and it was to be accomplished in a system of elementary and secondary schools intended to educate every school-age Catholic.

While the episcopal mandate never reached the goal of 100 percent participation, certainly the bishop's directives shaped Catholic church activity for the better part of a century. The two-year time frame specified in the council injunction proved to be overly optimistic. The actual number of schools increased from 2,464 in 1884 to 2,697 in 1886. The proportion of parishes sponsoring schools changed only slightly from 37 percent to 39 percent. Over time, though, Catholics came to support schools. About 60 percent of parishes sponsored elementary schools in the early sixties. Since school sponsorship tends to be associated with larger parishes, it is likely that the school program was available to much more than 60 percent of the American Catholic population.

The American bishops looked at their world in 1884 and selected the goal of a self-contained school system as the solution to provide religious education programs for school-age Catholics in the late nineteenth century. Catholics in 1997 need to look at their culture and make choices about the future of their religious education programs. Any view of the present state of the educational industry in the United States should include the following three patterns:

- The present Catholic school funding model, where parents pay tuition bills that increase far in excess of inflation, leads inevitably to a future where some good Catholic schools will educate some Catholics.
- Educational funding in the future will be constrained to growth patterns consistent with the rate of inflation.
- For a number of reasons ranging from bureaucratized management methods to urban decay, public education seems on the verge of significant innovation, where charter schools and tuition vouchers will lead to a dramatic restructuring of the present public education monopoly.

The mission of Catholic schools in the future must develop goal statements that deal with these three realities.

In November 1990, the American bishops published a document that comes close to being a useful mission statement for Catholic schools in our time. In a pastoral letter, *In Support of Catholic Elementary and Secondary Schools*, the bishops devised a mission statement designed to energize a flagging educational effort. They instructed that effort be made to make schools available to Catholic parents and that new initiatives, in both public and private sectors, be launched to secure financial assistance to accomplish this goal. The bishops then directed that strategies to accomplish these admirable goals be prepared for episcopal consideration no later than 1995.

Probably the glaring negative of the bishop's 1990 pastoral is that it continues the separate status of American Catholic church educational programming. In 1884, Catholic leaders wanted to protect their flock and consequently gave a strong affirmation at their Baltimore meeting for a self-contained school program. The bishops in 1990 seem to be suggesting that Catholic school managers need to work to bolster the operation of the separate-system educational model developed to fit the hostile religious circumstances of the last century. The 1990 episcopal letter talks of the successes of Catholic schools and the need for these programs almost as if public schools did not exist.

Perhaps now it is time to look at the entire American educational establishment and define Catholic schools in terms of circumstances that exist in our time. A critical factor in 1996 was the fact that the public educational monopoly teetered on the brink of significant innovation. For anyone who does not believe that our present public education monolith might actually change, consider the unfinished health care debate of recent years. For years doctors argued with the fervor of Moses throwing down stone tablets that the economic strategy of fee-for-service kept Americans free from the ravages of the socialized English medical model. It was not a durable argument. Rather, capitation with its implicit notion of rationing, is the present health-funding strategy. So, too, with education. American schools are changing and Catholic educational leaders should think of developing a mission statement to influence the outcome of that change.

Public school districts presently proscribe one program for their constituents from a central office. In the future, schools will organize around communities of interest and be managed at the building level according to district/state/city guidelines. The notion of parents picking a program that suits their family needs will determine the success or failure of any program. Frustration with a centrally managed public system has created an environment where a political leader like John Norquist, the Mayor of Milwaukee, helps lead a fight for school vouchers because he has lost confidence in public programs in his own city. "We have the most monopolistic school system in the world," he says. "It suppresses quality, is not customer-oriented, and is overly bureaucratic."[23] It is this demand for more responsive education programs that led the Wisconsin state legislature to fund tuition vouchers for poor students in the city of Milwaukee. The voucher program includes Lutheran and Catholic schools as potential recipients of a state-funded voucher. Should this rather unique program survive legal challenges, it offers an exceptional opportunity for Catholic leaders to rethink the mission of Catholic schools.

Wisconsin leaders designed the tuition voucher effort in Milwaukee to include 15,000 students at a cost of $39 million. Such a program hardly fits the definition of a pilot project. It also poses a fascinating question. How should this new approach to public educational management affect the mission of Catholic schools? One obvious response would be to ignore the change. If a Catholic school had an empty desk or two and the voucher reporting regulations were not too burdensome, so much the better. Otherwise, Catholic managers should pay no attention to a floundering public program and continue to provide a Catholic education to anyone who can afford the cost.

An alternative to the separate-system syndrome would entail thinking about the mission of Catholic schools. Who are the customers of Catholic programs? Catholics only? Non-Catholics looking for a culture that discusses the difference between right and wrong? The poor who may have no effective alternative? If you answered yes to all these questions, then Catholic schools cannot be paid for only from tuition. Actively pursuing tuition vouchers would be one strategy that would include more Catholics and the poor in Catholic school programs. The bishops instructed in 1990 that new initiatives be launched to secure financial assistance from public and private sectors. Perhaps it is time to take this admonition seriously and develop strategies that will provide Catholic educators with resources sufficient to accomplish a much more inclusive mission.

American Catholic schools need a new mission statement that focuses organizational energy in two specific directions. First, Catholics need to integrate their programs into the change that is confronting the public education industry in the form of tuition vouchers and 3,000 Federally-funded charter school programs. Second, Catholics must also look to their own community to find fiscal resources to support schools. In the past, the contributed services of women and men religious fueled the expansion of schools; for the future, Catholics must be persuaded to give more time and money to support religious education that is provided in school structures. In the next two sections of this research we will consider present efforts to seek tuition vouchers and the possibilities of greatly increasing Catholic giving. We want to explore strategies that could give life to a more inclusive mission statement for Catholic schools.

5. Take Tuition Vouchers Seriously

Catholic educators need to forge an alliance with the movement in this country advocating educational vouchers. Such programs represent an effort to restructure both public and private education by allowing parents an option of spending state-appropriated money to purchase an educational "product" of their choice. These programs seem to solve constitutional problems with separation of church and state and still afford the promise of significantly impacting Catholic school finances.

Current voucher efforts avoid the constitutional clash that canceled state aid programs in the 70s. Catholic schools mounted a successful effort in 1970 to secure state aid in Pennsylvania and Rhode Island. State legislatures voted to pay for the cost of teaching secular subjects in the Catholic system. The Supreme Court struck down the program in *Lemon v. Kurtzmann* when the justices determined that such programs constituted excessive entanglement between church and state. Writing for the majority, Chief Justice Warren Burger established a framework that has been cited as the standard to measure the legal status of any program.

First, the statute must have a secular legislative purpose; second, its principal or primary effect must be one that neither advances nor inhibits religion; finally, the statute must not foster excessive entanglement with religion...Our prior holdings do not call for total separation between church and state; total separation is not possible in an absolute sense. Some relationship is inevitable and the line of separation, far from being a wall, is a blurred, indistinct, and variable barrier depending on all the circumstances of a particular relationship.[24]

The justices saw the 1970s program of direct payments to schools as unconstitutional. Clearly they did not mean to preclude additional efforts. Justice Berger described the separation of church and state as blurred, indistinct and variable depending on all the circumstances. The present voucher movement avoids the problem of excessive entanglement by directing funding efforts to parents who may spend voucher funds on any approved program.

There is a temptation to look at voucher programs as constitutionally impractical, a modern-day version of jousting with windmills where a confused Don Quixote, ignoring the warning of his practical squire, Sancho Panza, charged into "fierce and unequal battle." For everyone raised to think of church-state relations as a chasm, Justice Berger's remarks about a blurred and indistinct connection depending on circumstances might come as a surprise. Catholic educational mission statements need to explore the opportunities offered by Lemon v. Kurtzman and support the development of strategies that could pass future court tests.

6. Double the Sunday Collection

American Catholics should adopt a goal to double the Sunday collection. We estimate total parish revenue for 1994 at $7.554 billion and the Sunday collection at $5.546 billion.[25] Parish elementary school subsidy for the 1994-95 school year amounted to $1.144 billion. Doubling the collection and keeping subsidy proportions constant would provide an infusion of $1.1 billion to the schools. This idea may sound like a pipe dream with little hope of realization. Solid evidence exists, however, to indicate that achieving such a Herculean goal may be practical. There were an estimated 18.2 million households registered in

Catholic parishes in 1991. Catholic household income was, on average, $40,879. The aggregate Catholic household income in 1991 was estimated at $744 billion. The actual Sunday collection for 1991 was estimated at $4.855 billion or .65 percent of household income. Doubling the Sunday collection would put Catholic giving at the approximate level of present contributions of Protestants to their various denominations.

An investigation of Catholic and Protestant giving shows that Catholics could increase giving. Protestants give much more to church programs than Catholics. In a paper on giving patterns, Professor Charles Zech of Villanova University investigated the differences between Protestant and Catholic giving. He asked: If a Catholic parish was of the same size, had the same clergy costs, exhibited the same attitudes, etc., as the typical Protestant congregation, would the contributions be the same as Protestants?

> *While in many cases Catholic parishes still rely on the weekly collection basket for their financial support, Protestants typically take a more formalized approach to stewardship, involving annual pledges, home visits to solicit pledges, and participatory budget-setting.*[26]

If it is true that sophisticated Protestant stewardship appeals are more effective that the Catholic collection basket, the gulf between Catholic and Protestant giving could be bridged when Catholics begin to implement such stewardship appeals. These appeals, if targeted to a need such as funding schools, could alter the present progression to a school system serving fewer and fewer Catholics.

7. Two Futures to Choose From

Catholic schools do succeed at providing efficient academic education and effective religious education. Enrollment has stabilized in recent years after more than two decades of precipitous declines. At least half of the American parent population rates public education as a negative or is, at best, worried about the effectiveness of public educational programs. Catholic elementary school programs presently generate 75 percent of program costs from program-specific activities like tuition and fund raising. Secondary schools function as virtual independent businesses by raising 92 percent of their program costs. These patterns all point in a single direction. Catholic elementary and secondary schools show every indication of surviving present problems and thriving into the foreseeable future. The $7.482 billion Catholic school program is not any more likely to fold than, say, IBM. Interestingly, the current situation of Catholic schools parallels the predicament of IBM, very successful and very struggling at the same time. Catholic school administrators must contend with both economic and organizational problems in determining the future involvement of the American Catholic church in the evolution of the United States educational industry.

The economic dilemma confronting school administrators developed as the composition and size of a school faculty changed radically. From the beginning of this century, Catholic schools expanded by relying on the contributed services of religious. A parish sponsored an elementary school where the pastor paid the convent grocery bill from the Sunday offerings of relatively poor immigrants. In addition, schools normally functioned in the sixties with a 35:1 pupil-teacher ratio. At the present time, schools operate with essentially lay faculties, an elementary pupil-teacher ratio of 17:1, and a secondary pupil-teacher ratio of 13:1. As a result of these changes, a typical parish elementary school probably costs about $653,000 to operate. This budget equals the total budget of the sponsoring parish. An average secondary school needed $2.38 million to pay bills for the 1996 school year. School leaders solved the economic problems of declining contributed services and shrinking class sizes by substituting rapidly escalating tuition programs for cost-saving measures that were effective for a previous generation. The effect of the economic redesign of schools may have contributed to the drop in the proportion of Catholics in Catholic schools from 47 percent in 1962 to about 19 percent at the present time.

An organizational problem facing administrators relates to the fact that the present system essentially functions with a theory of business designed to cope with anti-Catholic hostility prevalent in 1884. We suggest that Catholic program administrators need to adopt a three-part planning process defined by Peter Drucker in a 1994 issue of the Harvard Business Review. Drucker advocates that managers need to rethink assumptions about what is happening to the educational industry in the United States. Given a fresh look at the world, Catholic educators need to redefine the mission statement developed by American bishops at their Baltimore meeting in 1884. At that time, Catholics meant to defend themselves from the threat of Protestant encroachments. We need to find a mission that fits the current circumstances.

Two choices seem to be available. First, Catholic leaders can continue a system of schools designed to ignore the existence of public programs. The bishops meeting in Baltimore in 1884 clearly wanted to avoid the contaminating influence of Protestantism. Relying on the unique economic mechanism of contributed services of religious, Catholic leaders built a program that prided itself on having no contact with public programs. This program works and could continue to provide a Catholic education to those who can afford the cost of tuition. A second option open to Catholic administrators would be to design the future of Catholic education into innovations that promise to influence future public structures. Should Catholics actively pursue changes like tuition vouchers and charter schools, then the future of Catholic schools might include more middle-class, Hispanics and poor who presently cannot afford the escalating tuition charges.

Endnotes for Chapter 3

[1]   Andrew Greeley, "Catholic Schools: A Golden Twilight?" *America*, February 11, 1989, p. 106.

[2]   Reginald A. Neuwien, ed, *Catholic Schools in Action* (Notre Dame, IN: University of Notre Dame Press, 1966), p. 33.

[3]   Frank H. Bredeweg, CSB, *Catholic Elementary Schools and Their Finances–1979* (Washington, DC: National Catholic Educational Association, 1979), p.8.

[4]   Maryellen Schaub and David Baker, *Serving American Catholic Children & Youth* (Washington, DC: Department of Education, USCC, 1994), p. 14.

[5]   This statistic is part of the research prepared for this report and is the responsibility of the author. In general, all statistics referring to elementary and secondary school costs and revenue for the period 1987 through 1997 are estimates prepared by the author for this research report.

6   We estimate the cost of the average parish elementary school at $420,230 for 1989 and $184,372 for 1980. The average annual rate of change is calculated as follows: [($420,230/$184,372)x(.1111)]-1.

7   We estimate inflation growth according to the CPIU at 124 for 1989 and 82.4 for 1980. The average annual rate of inflation is calculated as follows: [(124/82.4)x(.1111)]-1.

8   We estimate tuition revenue for the average school at $208,515 for 1989 and $73,082 for 1980. The average annual rate of tuition increase is calculated as follows: [($208,515/$73,082)x(.1111)]-1.

9   Peter F. Drucker, "The Theory of Business," *Harvard Business Review*, September-October 1994, p. 95.

10   Ibid.

11   Jean Johnson, *Assignment Incomplete: The Unfinished Business of Educational Reform* (New York, NY: Public Agenda, 1995), p. 12.

12   Ibid., p. 12.

13   Ibid., p. 13.

14   Richard Lilly, "Schools Make the Grade," *The Seattle Times*, May 10, 1996, p. 1.

15   Neil Modie, "Education Rated as No. 1 of All State Issues," *The Post Intelligencer*, May 20, 1996, p. 1.

16   National Center for Educational Statistics, *Digest of Education Statistics*, 1995, U.S. Department of Education, Office of Educational Research and Improvement, NCES 98-029, October 1995, p. 34.

17   State of Washington, *Financial Reporting Summary for Fiscal 1995,* Office of Superintendent of Public Instruction, School Financial Services, Olympia, WA, Section 1, Statewide Average Financial Tables.

18   Neil G. McCluskey, SJ, *Catholic Education Faces Its Future* (Garden City, New York: Doubleday & Co., 1968), p. 48.

19   Ibid., p. 48.

20   Ibid., p. 50.

[21]   Ibid., p. 53.

[22]   Ibid., p. 56.

[23]   Editorial Comment, "A Genuine New Democrat," *Wall Street Journal*, March 21, 1996, p. A14.

[24]   David W. Kirkpatrick, *Choice in Schooling: A Case for Tuition Vouchers* (Chicago, Illinois: Loyola University Press, 1990), p. 80.

[25]   These estimates are derived from data developed for this project. The total for parish revenue is the result of the following calculation: (18,754 parishes) x ($402,800 average parish total revenue). Sunday collection is calculated as follows: (18,754 parishes) x ($295,740 average parish Sunday collection).

[26]   Peter A Zaleski and Charles E. Zech, "Economic and Attitudinal Factors in Catholic and Protestant Religious Giving," *Review of Religious Research*, vol. 36, no. 2 (1994), p. 165.

Chapter 4

Government and
Corporate Opportunities

– Dale McDonald, PBVM

The purpose of this presentation is to offer some suggestions about ways in which private schools may optimize the opportunities that are available for students and teachers to participate in federal education programs and in some of the private corporate funding initiatives available.

The federal programs that will be highlighted are the various Titles under Improving America's Schools Act (IASA), Goals 2000, E-Rate, Child Care Block Development Grants and legislation pertaining to professional development and technology.

Types of Programs

Federal government programs are usually one of two types: *discretionary* or *formula* grants.

a) Discretionary Grants:
These are awarded through a competitive process according to established criteria. Grant recipients are required to abide by various laws, regulations and executive orders that apply to recipients of federal funds.

If the listing of eligible applicants does not specify only public schools, private schools may be eligible to apply. Private schools also may be a member of a consortium as a nonprofit institution, but religious schools cannot receive direct grants of public funds (unlike hospitals and childcare agencies).

Information announcing competitions for discretionary grant programs of the U.S. Department of Education is published in the Federal Register. Information is also available at the U.S. Department of Education Web site: http://www.ed.gov.

b) Formula Grants:
These are grants of funds to the state or local education agency that are based on a predetermined formula, such as the number of children enrolled by grade or the number of children from low-income families. The formula requirements and procedures vary by program.

Participation of Private Schools Students in Federal Programs

Private schools may not receive direct aid from federal programs. The programs that include eligible private school children are rooted in the concepts of child benefit and public trusteeship. Child benefit assures that services are provided primarily to meet the needs of students and only incidentally for the schools they attend. The public trusteeship concept requires that the funds be paid to the "public trustees" (usually the local education agency) who use them to administer programs for all eligible children in the district.

Most of the federal programs are targeted to providing assistance to children in need, determined by a poverty-count formula. The criteria for determining the level of poverty of a family are based on the student eligibility for free and reduced-price lunch under the guidelines established by the U.S. Department of Agriculture. The school does not have to offer the lunch program—one must only determine if a student would be eligible for free or reduced-price lunch if the program were available in the school. The NCEA Web site provides information about various ways of collecting poverty data. Consult http://www.ncea.org and go to Public Policy, and then School Issues.

The Department of Agriculture administers the Federal School Lunch Program and publishes annual guidelines: http://www.usda.gov/fcs/cnp/ieg98-99.htm.

Working with the Public Trustees

Since the formula grant programs are administered by the LEA (local education agency/school district), it is important that private school administrators cultivate a close working relationship with the government program officers at the local district level. In addition to knowing which programs require "equitable participation of private school students," it is recommended that private school officials:

- Make sure their school and designated program coordinator is on the mailing list of the LEA and state education agency (SEA) so that notices will be received in a timely manner.

- Take an active part in the consultation process, finding out in advance the purpose of the programs and the criteria that are used to identify eligible children, teachers and other personnel for each program.

- Encourage the private school community—parents, teachers, administrators—to take an active role in assessing student needs and planning a program to meet those needs.

- Invite staff members and parent representatives to LEA and SEA meetings, as appropriate, to help in the discussion of student, teacher and other personnel needs.

- Be prepared to describe how the services being discussed will help meet the particular needs of the students, teachers and other personnel.

- Engage in early and frequent contact with public school officials so that public and private school officials are part of the consultation process throughout each phase of the project.

- Give the LEA a copy of the private school calendar, including starting and dismissal times, and notify the LEA as soon as possible of any unscheduled change in calendar.

- Resolve problems through personal contact and by following the chains of command in the public and private school systems. (adapted from *Serving Private School Students,* U.S. Department of Education, 1996)

ESEA/IASA (Improving America's Schools Act) Programs

Title I—Helping Disadvantaged Students Meet High Standards

In addition to the services provided directly to disadvantaged students, the law authorizes professional development opportunities that private schools personnel should utilize. Private school officials and staff who work directly with children participating in Title I programs and their parents, where appropriate, are to be included in professional development activities. If the LEA takes professional development funds "off the top," a proportionate amount is to be allocated for private schools. If professional development is part of the program expenditure, a proportionate share is to be provided for private school. The LEA has the responsibility for consulting with private school officials to prepare jointly a professional development plan that will meet the needs of participating private school personnel.

Title II—Dwight D. Eisenhower Professional Development Program

The amount of funds per student that an LEA provides for the benefit of private school teachers and students must be proportionately equal to the amount of funds per student that benefit the public school teachers. The programs should meet the needs of the private school teachers and students, and may be different from the public school program if the needs are different. A program which only allows private school personnel to fill open slots in public school programs does not fulfill the

LEA's responsibility. The private school officials should consult early on with the LEA to determine what type of programs should be developed to meet private school needs.

Title III—Technology for Education

Technology Literacy Grant: Under this program, The U.S. Department of Education makes formula grants to state education agencies (SEAs) which hold competitive grants bids and award grants to school districts for technology resources.

Technology Innovative Challenge Grant: Applications are submitted by an LEA to the U.S. Department of Education on behalf of a consortium of partners (one of which must be an LEA with a high percentage or number of children living below the poverty line). Private schools may be consortium members.

Under both programs, private school students and teachers must receive equitable benefits from the federal portion of the funds, as provided under Title XIV of ESEA, regardless of whether or not they were part of the consortium that made the application. Private school officials must be provided the opportunity, prior to the design of the program, to give input regarding the needs of private school students to be served by the project.

Title IV—Safe and Drug-Free Schools and Communities

Programs that can be supported by the Safe and Drug-Free Schools Program include mentoring, comprehensive health education, community service and service learning projects, conflict resolution, peer mediation and character education. The federal funds for private schools must be allocated on an equitable basis and require consultation between public and private school officials in the design and development of the program that will be funded. Private schools do not have to accept the district-wide program for public schools if they can demonstrate that the needs of their students are different from those being addressed by the public school program.

Title VI—Innovative Education Program Strategies

Services available for private schools include acquisition and use of instructional and educational materials, including library materials and computer software, provided they are secular, neutral and non-ideological. Services may provide technology training for teachers. Expenditures for private school students must be equal to those for public school children in all parts of the program except the new Class Size Reduction and Teacher Recruitment programs that are funded under Title VI. The law specifically excludes private school participation from all the benefits of these two programs, with the exception of professional development opportunities that a district might offer. However, the LEA is not required to use any of the funds for professional development but instead, may spend all of the funds on teacher recruitment, testing and certification.

Goals 2000: Educate America Act

As part of the education reform movement, this act provides funds to states and school districts to develop high standards and quality assessments for students and training and professional development program for teachers.

Participation of private school students and staff is limited, but some benefits are available. Private school officials may request information regarding education goals, state standards, student performance standards, curriculum materials and state assessments developed with Goals 2000 funds from the SEA and LEA. In addition, professional development opportunities supported by Goals 2000 funds must be made available to teachers and administrators in private schools in proportion to the number of students attending private schools in the state.

While the burden of initiating requests is on private school officials, private school personnel must be cognizant of the information about program development and recent trends. They can receive this material without cost to assist in the school's long-range planning efforts.

Child Care and Development Block Grant

The Child Care and Development Block Grant (CCDBG), administered by the U.S. Department of Health and Human Services, funds state efforts to provide quality child care services for low-income family members who work, train for work or attend school. CCDBG provides funding to help low-income families access quality childcare for their children. Funds granted to parents/guardians are available in the form of certificates, grants and contracts for child care services. Certificates can be used for public or private, religious or nonreligious and center or home-based care. Pre-K school-based programs are eligible to receive CCDBG certificates from parents. It is important to inform parents/guardians of these opportunities, because often the social workers do not inform then, but instead tend to channel clients into day-care centers. For general information about the CCDBG program, contact the Child Care Bureau at the U.S. Department of Health and Human Services at http://www.acf.dhhs.gov

Research and Professional Development
Higher Education Act

The most recent reauthorization of the Higher Education Act (HEA) provides for the equitable inclusion of private school teachers and administrators in post-secondary programs related to professional development and teacher preparation. If a college or university receives grants to conduct these programs under HEA, private school personnel must be given equitable opportunity to participate along with public school teachers and administrators.

Programs of college loan forgiveness for teaching in schools in high poverty areas or subject areas deemed to have a teacher shortage have been extended to include eligible private and religious school teachers. Private school teachers may qualify for a Perkins loan forgiveness if they are teaching full-time in a school designated as eligible by the SEA. Detailed information about the program is available on the Department of Education Web site: http://www.ed.gov.

The site does not mention eligibility of private school teachers but do not be dissuaded—the law does apply.

The National Library of Education

The National Library of Education (NLE) is the largest federally-funded library in the world devoted solely to education. It houses, at the US Department of Education, more than 200,000 books and about 750 periodical subscriptions in addition to studies, reports, Educational Resources Information Center (ERIC) microfiche, and CD-ROM databases. Internet users may access and download U.S. Department of Education resources and information, including legislation, publication summaries and full texts, grant information, datasets and ERIC. Information is available at http://www.ed.gov/NLE.

The Regional Educational Laboratory Program

The Regional Educational Laboratory Program is the U.S. Department of Education's largest research and development program. Administered by the Office of Educational Research and Improvement (OERI), the network of 10 regional labs provides information regarding the best available research and knowledge from practice to further educational reform.

A listing of the regional labs and their specialty areas can be found at their homepage: http://www.nwrel.org/national.

Regional Technology in Education Consortia

The R*TEC program is established to help educators successfully integrate technology into K-12 classrooms and other educational settings. The R*TECs establish and conduct regional activities that address professional development, technical assistance and information resource dissemination to promote the effective use of technology in education, with special emphasis on meeting the documented needs of educators and learners in the region they serve. Consult their Web site: http://rtec.org.

Technology Programs

Transfer of Excess and Surplus Federal Computer Equipment

The Computers for Learning program donates surplus federal computer equipment to schools and educational nonprofits, giving special consideration to those with the greatest need. Private as well as public schools are eligible for materials for use in pre-K through 12th grade. The Computers for Learning Web site allows schools and educational nonprofits to register quickly and easily to request surplus federal computer equipment. Federal agencies use the Web site to donate computers to schools and educational nonprofits.

To find out what is available and how to participate consult the Web site: http://www.computers.fed.gov.

Universal Service Fund "E-Rate" Telecommunications Discounts

The Telecommunications Act of 1996 provides students with access to the vast educational resources on the Information Superhighway through the universal service fund discount program know as the E-Rate. The chief program characteristics are:

- All public and private nonprofit K-12 schools with endowments less than $50 million and public libraries are eligible for discounts.

- Discounts apply to all commercially available telecom services, including telephone, Internet access and internal connections, including wireless, wired and cable.

- Discounts range from 20% to 90%, based on the number of students eligible for the federal school lunch program.

- Discounts also apply to equipment necessary to transport information within a school or library, including routers, hubs, network file servers (and necessary software) and LANs.

- Discounts do not apply to computers (except for network file servers), other hardware, software, fax machines, modems, teacher training, upgrades to the electrical system and asbestos removal.

- Applications are processed on a first-come, first-served basis—but within a 75-day window that allows all applications received within the announced time period to be treated as all having been received on the same day.

During the first year, the E-Rate fund provided more than $1.4 billion to applicants who filed within the application window. Funding to cover internal connections requests reached down to the 70% discount level. Catholic schools have received significant funding commitments—particularly schools in the high-end discount ranges because they received internal connections funding. One school received more than $400 thousand, another $200 thousand and many in the tens of thousands.

The application period for the second year of E-Rate grants opened on December 1, 1998 and extended to April 6, 1999. For a review of the program, consult the NCEA Web site: http://www.ncea.org and go to Telcom Act in the Index. You will find current and background information, guidelines for calculating your discount and materials related to technology plans. Consult the E-Rate Web site: http://www.slcfund.org for the latest information, including downloadable forms and lists of recipients by state. The EdLiNC Web site is a useful resource as well.

TIIAP

The Telecommunications and Information Infrastructure Assistance Program (TIIAP) is a highly competitive, merit-based grant program that brings the benefits of an advanced national information infrastructure to communities throughout the United States. TIIAP provides matching grants to nonprofit organizations such as schools, libraries, hospitals, public safety entities and state and local governments. Grants are used to fund projects that improve the quality of, and the public's access to, education, health care, public safety and other community-based services.

The grants may be used to purchase equipment for connection to networks, including computers, video conferencing systems, network routers and telephones; to buy software for organizing and processing all kinds of information, including computer graphics and databases; to train staff, users and others in the use of equipment and software; to purchase communications services, such as Internet access; to evaluate the projects; and to disseminate the project's findings.

State and local governments, colleges and universities and non-profit entities are eligible to apply. Although individuals and for-profit organizations are not eligible to apply, they may participate as project partners. Grant recipients under this program will be required to provide matching funds toward the total project cost. Applicants must document their capacity to provide matching funds. Matching funds may be in the form of cash or in-kind contributions.

While religious activities cannot be the essential thrust of a grant, an application will not be ineligible where sectarian activities are only incidental to the overall project purpose for which funding is requested. For further information contact TIIAP: http://www.ntia.doc.gov.

Corporate Foundations and Philanthropies

There is a wealth of resources available for educators who are looking for funding for special projects or technology innovations in schools. Note, however, that most of these grants will not fund regular operational activities and capital improvements for schools.

Available information about resources generally falls into two categories: a) finding sources of funding from government or private entities and b) help in writing a proposal that will actually get funded.

Resources for Locating and Obtaining Funding

On-line sources

The Internet and World Wide Web are excellent places to research grants. In addition to the timeliness of the information, on-line sites frequently provide application forms and an e-mail link to obtain further information and assistance. The following are typical of the kinds of resources one might find available on-line:

http://web.fie.com/cws/sra/resource.htm. This site provides links to both federal and private funding sources with information about grant databases, proposal development tools, etc.

http://www.educationnetwork.com/grant.htm. This site includes links, resources and services all aimed at helping your organization get the funding it needs.

http://www.grantwriters.com. This site is organized into four parts: 1) free information about what is new in the grant-writing world; 2) the bookstore: a source for the best in grant writing materials including books, guides and diskettes loaded with sample documents; 3) training opportunities, including open workshops, on-site programs, university courses and Web-based instruction; 4) commercial services to guide proposal writing.

Publications

Aid for Education is a newsletter published twice a month which lists private and federal funding opportunities. An annual subscription Is $259 and may be ordered form CD Publications, 8204 Fenton Avenue, Silver Spring, MD 20910.

Funding Update is a monthly newsletter provides information about funding sources and purposes, eligibility requirements, contact names, etc. It may be obtained from the Grant Resource Center at Santa Clara County Education Department, (408) 453-6691, for $69 per year.

Finding Funding: Grantwriting and Project Management From Start to Finish is a comprehensive book that contains sections about writing proposals, finding funding sources, implementing projects and ongoing evaluations and assessments. It is available from Corwin Press, (805) 499-9774.

Proposal Writing Hints

1. Grants are usually targeted to specific purposes, projects or classifications (math education, at-risk children, school-to work training, etc.) that are of primary interest to the corporation or foundation. Find out what the interests of the corporations are before applying.

2. Many corporations and foundations target their grants locally. They want some type of local community involvement in the geographic area of the corporate headquarters, and more frequently, they choose to serve areas where they have large numbers of their employees.

3. Scan the horizon: consult with corporations and businesses in your area; find out what they offer.

4. Tailor applications to meet specific objectives of the program-funding criteria: broaden your horizons and expand the scope of your objectives to incorporate theirs in what you want to do.

5. Decide who is best suited to apply—a local school, diocese, consortium of public-private-community groups. It is often better to align different community interests to make the strongest case.

6. It is imperative that applicants seek advice from people who know how to access the programs that are available. Obtain professional help in writing applications, especially in the beginning.

Conclusion

There are many opportunities available for private school teachers and administrators to access for improving the quality of teaching and learning for all students. However, it appears that two factors militate against greater Catholic school participation in existing programs which are mandated to include private school students and staff:

1. Lack of information, since the U.S. Department of Education does not publicize the opportunities for equitable participation of private school students in its general advertising campaigns. This results in assumptions that such opportunities are nonexistent. Many local school districts are unaware of the applicability of specific federal programs and/or the regulations which are supposed to guide their trusteeship of the public funds.

   It is imperative that private school administrators know these regulations and know the channels of recourse they may pursue if equity is not observed.

   Information about private school participation in federally funded programs is contained in the publication of the Office of Non-Public Education, U.S. Department of Education, *Serving Private School Students with Federal Programs* (1996). The publication and other relevant information pertaining to private schools and applicable federal government programs many be found on the Web site: http://www.ed.gov/offices/OIIA/NonPublic/about.html.

2. Insufficient personnel: Already overworked personnel at the diocesan and school levels frequently do not have the time to deal with cumbersome paperwork and inter-personal relationships that need to be cultivated with the numerous local educational agencies (LEAs) that control federal programs, or the time and expertise to develop grant proposals.

   However daunting, these are challenges which must be tackled if Catholic school students are to continue to receive the high quality education needed to live in an increasingly technology- and information-rich world. The good news is that there are many resources available to help schools if educators have the vision and determination to find them and to build partnership to obtain them.

Chapter 5

Successful Development Initiatives

– Mary E. Tracy, SNJM

Like bicycles, Catholic school development programs can be designed in many and varied ways. Some may resemble high-powered mountain bikes capable of climbing rough terrain; several may look like manual, no-speed bikes; a few could parallel recumbent bikes which allow the driver a relaxing no-impact ride. Of course, regardless of the unique institutional characteristics, most Catholic school development programs are improving steadily, creating more predictable and greater results.

Occasionally, a major obstacle or system flaw requires the school leaders to fix the bicycle even while riding it. When an advancement program has been in operation for several years, many Catholic school development professionals find themselves in the complex and dubious position of needing to fix the bike in order to keep riding. Staffing can be limited, budget constraints are real, technology is expensive, only to become outdated in eighteen months, and the institutional need for substantially greater income from the development program is clear. An institutional time of shifting gears in the development system provides the opportunity to apply more creativity and ingenuity to that which already is optimum. The possibility of achieving even greater results—riding up a higher slope—is always before us. The process of reflection, design and implementation can be as exhilarating as the outcome.

Realistically, then, what should the effective Catholic school development program look like? Eleven characteristics are presented here to be used as guidelines in designing a program or as a standard against which to measure a current program.

1. The goal is money. Yes, one needs to spend money to make money and friend-raising is vital but the ultimate goal is money. Development goals should be presented in terms of net funds generated.

2. Annual giving, exclusive of special events, should be viewed as the primary annual development program, the one that has unlimited potential to grow in volume and in gift size. Strive to raise 8-10% of operating revenue through the annual fund. The annual fund should be a 12-month comprehensive, solicitation-based program.

3. The school should plan to implement capital campaigns at regular intervals and have a clear understanding of the complementary relationship between the annual fund and the capital campaign.

4. Long-range planning should serve as the appropriate context for goal-setting in the development program. An annual development plan should be produced outlining expected achievement in annual fund, capital gift acquisition, planned gifts and special events. This plan should be written and approved by the development committee of the board.

5. Major gifts are strategies for the annual fund or capital campaign. A strong major-gifts program should be developed to benefit the annual fund, capital campaign and special projects. While careful attention is given to all aspects of the development program, a particular focus should be on major gifts.

6. Constituency giving for the annual fund should grow steadily. The board must give first, and at 100%. Goals for the other constituencies of parents, past parents, grandparents, alumni, members of senior class or eighth grade, pastors, coaches, faculty/staff and corporate/foundation gifts should be set accordingly. The focus groups for the annual fund are more inclusive than only the parents or only the alumni.

7. The comprehensive development program should be in operation all the time: the annual fund timeline is from July 1 to June 30 (or adjusted to correspond to the fiscal year) and capital campaign solicitation takes place most intensely in the pre-campaign and early stages, but never stops until the victory is celebrated. And at that point, it will be time to gear up for the next campaign.

8. The head of school should be a regular solicitor of gifts—for the annual fund as well as for the capital campaign. In addition to the head of the school and the board chairperson, selected board members and selected volunteers are to be consistent solicitors of gifts. The solicitors need technical training, coaching and supervision from the head of the school, the board chairperson and the development director.

   Depending on the expectations of the institution and the preferences of the school's head, the director of development is not typically a solicitor of gifts. She/he is responsible for organizing the fund-raising efforts of others, for completing donor and prospect research and for keeping track of all contacts and results.

9. A planned giving program, either preliminary or highly developed, is an essential component of a complete development program. Even in a one-person shop, figure out ways to educate the constituencies on planned gift opportunities and present compelling options—in relationship as well as in print.

10. The development office requires professional staffing. At least one full-time development director and one full-time (or part-time, if necessary) administrative assistant are essential. Depending on the size of the alumni records and donor base, a database manager may be needed in addition to the administrative assistant. In schools with long histories and extensive alumni bases, an alumni coordinator is needed to see that reunions occur regularly and standard alumni events take place and are of a high quality. The development director should focus on solicitation-based giving, not on special events.

11. Publications are central to the development operation. These should be produced by a skilled professional at a reasonable budgetary level. In some schools, publications are outsourced, but this method still requires internal drafting and proofreading—always extensive proofreading.

Most of the steps to designing an excellent development program can be implemented incrementally. Careful planning for the program development would clarify appropriate timelines and budgetary factors. The involvement of volunteers in the creation of the plan—board members, committee members, parents and alumni—creates an inner circle of shareholders who are ready to implement the plan. People support what they create.

The experience itself of constructing the Catholic school development program becomes as important as the final product. The creativity, the teamwork, the imagination and the faith-sharing relate directly to the mission of the Catholic school. And the results speak for themselves.

Chapter 6

Creatively Financing Catholic Schools: A Perspective from Donors and Foundations

– Francis J. Butler

At the outset I congratulate Regina Haney and Fr. Joe O'Keefe for the choice of topics for this year's SPICE Institute. Your development work—rooted in a sound concept of stewardship—is not only vital for the schools you represent but a gift to the whole church. Whenever and wherever people are helped to see how stewardship and faith connect, wider participation in the church's mission ultimately follows.

My topical assignment is somewhat daunting by virtue of its magnitude. I am to reflect with you on the wide world of Catholic philanthropy and Catholic education. Given the fact that the members of the Foundations and Donors Interested in Catholic Activities (FADICA) represent nearly 200 million dollars in annual donations and you represent over a half billion dollars in educational activity, I feel compelled to narrow the scope of my remarks so that I leave you with some concrete ideas of where foundation funding actually might be found. No doubt there are a few of you who came into this room with the famed passage from the movie Jerry McGuire burning in your brain: "Show me the money!"

Those of you who might have read the February/March edition of NCEA's journal *Momentum* will recognize that Catholic schools have indeed captured the attention of Catholic philanthropists in an unprecedented way. In an article, "Catholic Education and Catechesis: A Light in the City," I reported on FADICA's recent discussions on Catholic inner-city schools. Joe O'Keefe, Len DeFiore, John Convey and a host of others were present when we brought together our foundations and several innovative Catholic inner-city schools and business-led educational foundation projects. I would like to draw from that discussion later in this presentation.

First, however, I would like to cite a few examples of where donors are signaling their strong interest in Catholic education. You will be hearing more about these programs and others during the course of the next four days.

- One of my favorite examples of how foundations have become new partners in Catholic education is the University of Notre Dame's Alliance for Catholic Education Program.

- Having successfully fielded well over 100 new Catholic school teachers, ACE demonstrates that school-related service learning in a Catholic setting can attract and retain spiritually motivated and talented young people to the profession of teaching. As you may know, ACE has not only received substantial multi-year commitments from several Catholic foundations but from larger secular foundations, and from the Learn and Serve America program under the Corporation for National Service.

- Boston College's Urban Teachers' Corps, though newer and more geographically bound, is showing similar promise. Thanks to major gifts from two Catholic foundations here in Boston, Boston College will offer new teachers an opportunity to gain classroom experience in the inner-city under the mentorship of seasoned Catholic educators.

- The University of Notre Dame also reports the formation of the Institute for Educational Initiatives. It is made possible through major grants and will serve two purposes: 1) to award a master's degree in education through its applied educational programs next year and 2) conduct school-related research.

- With grants from private foundations, The University of Dayton has begun the Lalann Program—a teachers' corps developed by Dayton's new Center for Catholic Education. The program has started with half a dozen teacher graduates who will begin serving in schools in the Archdiocese of Cincinnati this fall. Dayton has also begun the PACE Scholarship Program, enabling 1,000 students to receive $1,000 each in scholarship assistance to attend a school of their choice in the Dayton area.

- Corporate-led charitable foundations for Catholic school support are emerging nearly everywhere. The largest of its kind is in Los Angeles. The archbishop's Education Foundation, established a decade ago, provides in excess of $6 million yearly in direct subsidies for Catholic schools. It has an endowment of $85 million. Some 26 private foundations have given $5 million in tuition grants and 16 foundations have given $25 million for the endowment.

Where there are large concentrations of Catholic urban schools, you will find similar efforts. In Milwaukee for example, business, community and foundation leaders raise $4.5 million a year to support scholarship aid for Catholic school students.

You may find similar undertakings across the country in Baltimore, Philadelphia, Detroit, and Chicago, Dayton, Brooklyn, Buffalo, Indianapolis, to name just a few areas.

- Foundations are helping Catholic schools in indirect ways, too. The Lilly Endowment has a long history of support for education-related research. In the recent past, it has awarded a one half million dollar collaborative research project to The Catholic University of America to complete a compendium study of all present research on Catholic schools.

- Several members of FADICA mark their fifth year of working with Boston College in bringing about the Spiritual Growth Institute. This 10-day program is a retreat and skills-sharpening exercise designed to help primarily Catholic inner-city school teachers as they discuss the vocation of teaching and explore the world of moral and spiritual development in the classroom. This summer, with the help of the NCEA, a process got underway, training teachers to conduct local versions of the program in all areas of the country.

Later in your program you will be hearing about several other very impressive projects—the WIN program for Inner-city Schools in the Rochester diocese, stewardship initiatives in the Diocese of Wichita, the Campaign for Elementary School Endowments in Toledo, the Bison Foundation in Buffalo, and a number of other measures.

The projects that I have just mentioned are presented to you as examples of where foundations are showing their intensified interest in Catholic education. The projects demonstrate specifically how Catholic education is attracting new philanthropic dollars and countless hours of volunteer service.

Abstracting from these programs for a moment, we might be able to see what attracted foundation backing.

- It is clear that programs like ACE, the Urban Teachers Corps, and the Dayton program are not only investing in the future of teaching itself, but they are explicitly spiritually based, and they help the church engage young adults in its ministry to the poor.

- Research projects like the Catholic University study, new centers for education at Notre Dame, the work here at Boston College (including this Institute) and at the University of Dayton are providing powerful tools for tracking educational excellence and faith-based learning. There is no substitute for solid study and research.

Whether you seek to broaden community support for Catholic schools or are talking with a Catholic foundation, you are finding that today's donor is result-oriented and demands measurable evidence for claims of excellence.

- Teaching for Spiritual Growth is addressing in an innovative way the vocation of teaching itself, its prayerful and moral underpinnings, and is showing how love and listening are essential to finding God in the classroom.

- Initiatives to form school foundations, like the one in Los Angeles that I mentioned offer exciting ways to broaden public interest in the schools. They also benefit the larger church by developing lay leadership, ecumenical understanding and community concern.

So far I have mentioned teacher service corps programs, research, teacher training and new business led foundations. But I believe that there are still particular problems that are drawing more attention and more interest on the part of Catholic foundations, because research is showing them to be of strategic importance to the future of parochial education in the cities.

In our meeting last summer, John Convey of Catholic University told our foundations that there were six special areas of major concern for Catholic urban schools.

Most obvious are the severe financial problems of these institutions. Urban Catholic schools are almost always associated with parishes that just can't support them; they must, therefore, charge substantially higher tuition than other schools located in more affluent parts of the diocese; often urban schools have large amounts of uncollected tuition. Most of these schools are in buildings that need serious capital improvement.

Second, urban Catholic schools consistently struggle with enrollment due to student mobility and unstable neighborhoods. This has enormous implications for budgets and staffing and often leave these schools in hazardous circumstances.

Third, leadership is often lacking. A healthy school requires a strong administrative team where pastors and principals work together. While examples of strong principals and supportive pastors abound, nonetheless, major resources are needed for management and leadership training.

Fourth, Dr. Convey told us that urban Catholic schools often lack a strategic plan and operate on an ad hoc basis hoping year-by-year to get by. Without a plan of some kind, the longer-range outlook for the survival of such institutions is unfavorable.

The issue of governance is a particularly vexing one for Catholic schools in urban areas. Too often these schools lack nurturing/sponsoring arrangements and active advisory boards that help the school raise funds, plan, set goals and measure progress.

Perhaps most fundamental of all is the research that shows that many urban Catholic schools are either grappling with or neglecting the question of what it means to be Catholic. As you know, it is far more than a problem of how many students of Catholic faith are served. It is about mission, culture, people, environment, rituals, curricula and the ethos of the school.

A strongly religious culture in the school is the one factor that more and more Catholic foundations consider to be the best predictor of long term success.

These six areas—finances, enrollment, leadership, planning, governance and identity—suggest prime topics where foundations are very apt to participate with Catholic educators.

Let's look for a moment at each one of them to see how they might figure in grant proposals you yourself might be developing:

Finances
Generally speaking, foundations are going to be attracted to development efforts that benefit more than just one school. This suggests the question: Is there at present an overall development effort in your area led by business, foundation and community leaders? More and more this seems to be an essential building block of school development. It fosters a spirit of stewardship and cooperation among the schools while educat-

ing the broader public on its work. Grant-making foundations were once adverse to underwriting development programs. Now they are beginning to look at them as activities that build capacity rather than viewing them as overhead.

Foundations recognize that they will have lasting impact on the schools while increasing the constituency for them.

Enrollment and Planning

Within your individual school, foundations would ask: Are you making creative use of the media to tell your story and to broaden your potential student pool? How do you identify potential students? What are your enrollment projections for the next three years? How do you present the school to the parish or to other churches? Do you publish an annual report? Do you have any kind of event where outstanding students are given recognition, awards or scholarships in a public ceremony? Each year two members of FADICA confer scholarship grants for outstanding student achievement. It is a great communications strategy that provides a very personal and effective way for the schools to engage the attention and interest of major donors.

Leadership and Governance

Foundations are interested in whether schools are planning for the future by investing in leadership development. Have you done an inventory of the leadership skills of your parents, alumni and friends?

Would you or your fellow teachers be willing to draw from the expertise of local business schools or companies for management and operations advice? Would you pioneer some creative ways to strengthen the administration of your school? What are you doing now by way of in-service training for your teachers? Are you taking advantage of any of the new mentoring opportunities that programs like ACE, the Urban Teachers Corps or Jesuit Volunteers offer? If not, foundations might be able to help.

Religious Identity

Is this taken for granted in your school or are you making conscious efforts to explore the meaning of being a Catholic institution in everything that you do? How are the faith literacy needs of your faculty met, for example? Are teacher and student retreats held on a regular basis? How is the spiritual life of your teachers and students nourished?

These days we need to think of Catholicism as a spiritual path and build experiential bridges for young people linking them to community service. How a school does this is most important. If it is done as a random affair, it is one thing. But if such experiences are enriched by social and ethical reflection and spiritual grounding, they can reinforce the religious culture of the entire school. We have only just begun to explore service learning in the wider church and inceptive thinking on the part of Catholic educators is very welcome.

In singling out these six subjects for grant appeals, I don't want to imply that creativity is not already at work in your development plans. You will hear plenty of examples during the next few days. All I am suggesting is that foundations often think strategically, looking at generic problems and then finding ways to solve them. In the best examples of philanthropy, foundation trustees are told to view themselves as change agents. They discuss and evaluate their own work in terms of broad challenges facing the church. Let me illustrate what I mean.

Professor Scott Appleby, Director of the Cushwa Center for the Study of American Catholicism, recently addressed the Catholic foundation community on the subject of generation transition. Young people, unlike their parents, are being formed not so much in the old triangle of church, school, neighborhood/home, but in the triangle of popular culture, the market place and electronic media.

This has presented the church with enormous challenges in inculcating in young Catholics its traditions, beliefs and values. "Young people don't see their faith as a whole. They may have a little bit of this or that, but they do not understand the tradition as a whole."

(Parenthetically, just last week, Monika Hellwig of the ACCU remarked in an opening address at Iona College that to date Catholic colleges have not done an effective job in drawing students into the social teachings of the church. At this same conference, Archbishop John Roach remarked, "Part of the problem is that young people are raised with a preoccupation of obtaining material success and subjects that don't help them find a lucrative job after graduation are deemed irrelevant.")

So here we have a generation in transition that is on the one hand spiritually hungry, but on the other hand copiously inactive in Sunday worship and astonishingly inarticulate about their own faith tradition. This is what I mean by a major problem. For Catholic foundations such problems provide a kind of landscape from which the work and value of individual ministries may be judged. Let's consider how Catholic schools would be viewed up against the generation challenge that I mentioned.

Research shows that no other church institution, including the parish has so thoroughly and effectively touched and formed the minds and behavior of young people as Catholic schools.

Research confirms that leaders of tomorrow's church—our priests, religious and active laity—will continue to be graduates of Catholic schools.

One bishop remarked recently at St. Johns University, "The Catholic school system in America can be singled out as the one factor leading to the vitality and strength of the Catholic church in the United States." Andrew Greeley's research shows that Catholic schools not only produce church leaders but bring about more happiness and confidence among their graduates, support for the equality of women, generosity and awareness of the complexity of moral decision making, and higher intellectual achievement.

We live in a time of declining child well being, the continuing disintegration of the family, a growing sense that relations between the races, economic classes and generations are not guided by shared understanding. We live in a time marked by a coarseness and harshness in popular culture; a time when success is measured by how much money we have; a time when there has been a dramatic undermining of the distinction between right and wrong.

Catholic schools are the seedbeds for virtuous leadership in the next century, both within our church and in the broader society.

They are places where research has proved that moral and religious understanding essential to human flourishing is reaching the next generation. And that is precisely how to present your case to foundations. Your institutions are remarkable investments for the future.

This past month, FADICA gathered for its annual meeting. Our subject was higher education and Catholic intellectual life. As you can imagine in the post-modern deconstructionism world of the academy, the Catholic intellectual tradition is an endangered species. Yet there is emerging on many campuses the groundwork for a whole new generation of Catholic scholarship.

There are new Catholic study centers, for example, forums for research and interdisciplinary dialogue, mentoring and spiritual formation programs for faculty and mission-related hiring. All of these measures augur well for the future.

Catholic scholarship will be taken seriously if the best and brightest minds, influenced by the most deeply committed hearts, enter the world of higher education and research. But one could argue that this all begins with your work as you form the scholars of tomorrow.

What an imposing challenge! How pivotal are Catholic schools today as gateways to the church's future.

I cannot imagine why you wouldn't engage Catholic foundations in the exciting work that you do.

Chapter 7

Creatively Resourcing Catholic Schools: The Critical Issue of Hiring and Retaining High Quality Teachers

– Joseph M. O'Keefe, SJ

The most important resource in a school is its faculty, and in this regard Catholic educators face some daunting challenges in the near future. This chapter begins with an investigation of teacher availability for public schools in the United States. It then examines the impact of an impending teacher shortage on Catholic schools. Next, it describes some current programmatic initiatives that address resourcing needs in these institutions. Finally it considers other ways in which the Catholic community can more creatively resource its schools in the future.

Teacher Availability in the United States

At a recent trustees' meeting at a prestigious Catholic high school, the principal reported on the difficulty of attracting new teachers for the upcoming academic year. Though the salary and benefit package is very good compared to others in the Catholic sector, the school cannot match the strong financial incentives that the Commonwealth of Massachusetts is offering to talented prospective teachers. Massachusetts is not alone in offering such incentives. According to *Education Week* (Archer, 1998), Alabama is offering $1,500 a year for the 10-year life of the certificate; California, a $10,000 one-time bonus; Delaware, $1,500 a year for the 10-year life of the certificate; Florida, a pay increase equal to 10 percent of the average teacher's salary in the state for the life of the certificate; Georgia, a 5 percent pay increase; Iowa, $10,000 a year for five years; Kentucky, approximately $2,000 in a one-time bonus; Mississippi, $6,000 a year for the life of the certificate; North Carolina, a 12 percent annual bonus for the life of the certificate; Ohio, a $2,500 annual bonus for the life of the certificate; Oklahoma, a $5,000 annual bonus for the life of the certificate; South Carolina and Wisconsin, a $2,000 one-time bonus. Among other incentives are housing bonuses in Baltimore matched with an income-tax break in Maryland. New York State, which will hire at least 30,000 teachers in the next five years, has begun recruiting in Europe (Bradley, 1998).

Along with the state initiatives mentioned above, public schools will benefit from recent federal legislation aimed at staffing public schools (Riley, 1999), tuition grant and mentorship programs sponsored by teachers' unions (National Education Association, 1999) and private non-profit organizations such as Recruiting New Teachers, Inc. Recruiting New Teacher's Urban Teacher Collaborative is a good example. It offers national recruitment and referral network as well as local recruitment, retention and support efforts at urban colleges and school districts. It has created improved career corridors for individuals underrepresented in teaching, improved information and communications via a teacher-recruitment, development and diversity toolkit and improved communications and support through conferences, newsletters, state-wide initiatives and other teacher development activities.

The law of supply and demand has forced many public school districts to be more flexible in hiring practices. According to the National Commission on Teaching and America's Future (1999), more than 12 percent of all newly hired teachers enter the workforce without any training at all, and another 15 percent enter without having fully met state standards. More than 50,000 people who lack formal training have entered teaching annually on emergency or substandard licenses. According to a 1997 survey conducted by the National Center For Education Information (Feistritzer, 1998b), 35 states report that interest in alternative teacher certification has increased in the last five years and 24 states report that state legislators have shown greater interest in alternative teacher certification. Half the states report that the number of individuals getting licensed to teach through alternative routes has increased in the last five years.

Why are policy-makers so concerned about teacher recruitment? Though there are contesting opinions (Feistritzer, 1998a), most people believe that in the next decade schools in the United States will hire 2.2 million new teachers (United States Department of Education, 1999). During the same time frame, the number of teachers will increase by 14 percent (National Center for Educational Statistics, 1998). According to a recent report published by Recruiting New Teachers, Inc. (1999), three factors contribute to this condition. First, the teacher workforce is aging. More than one-third of teachers in the USA are over 48. In the next ten years, a large portion of the nation's teacher workforce will retire—precisely at the moment when student enrollment reaches near-historic highs. Second, changing student enrollment will necessitate new hiring. By 2006, schools will educate 54.6 million children, almost 3 million more than today. The need for teachers will follow this demographic bulge as it moves through elementary and high school into college in the early years of the 21st century. Third, most school reform efforts call for decreased student-teacher ratios. For example, California asked its 5,000 elementary schools to cut the size of classes in primary grades from an average of 30 students per class to 20. To accomplish this goal, the state will need to hire 20,000 new teachers, a challenge it has had difficulty meeting.

The shortage is most acute in urban districts. According to Recruiting New Teachers, Inc., three-fourths (77%) of urban school districts often suffer shortages in high-need areas, including mathematics, science, special education, bilingual education and elementary education. About two-thirds of urban districts allow non-certified teachers to teach under an emergency license while four in ten allow for hiring of long-term substitutes. More than half the districts need more full-time elementary teachers. There is high need for male teachers (85%) and teachers of color (92%). The problem of recruitment is compounded by the fact that many new teachers leave the field. On the national level, 30 percent of teachers leave within the first five years; the figure is much higher in urban districts (Draper, 1999).

Education policy makers have voiced their concern about this phenomenon and offered new initiatives. For example, Richard Riley, United States Secretary of Education (1999) made the following comments about the public school teacher shortage:

- Low salaries are a very real problem. I ask public officials to recognize—sooner rather than later—that we aren't going to be able to get good teachers on the cheap any more.

- We really do need to take a comprehensive look at established rules about the portability of pensions, credentials and years in service. The current maze of disconnected state laws has become a significant drawback to keeping good teachers in the profession in our increasingly mobile society.

- Our colleges of education simply must be supported in reaching for a new level of rigor. I urge colleges of education to move swiftly to create many more clinical experiences for their students. Future teachers need to be learning how to teach alongside master teachers.

- I also encourage many more states to follow California's lead in creating a broad system of support for first-time teachers. We give new teachers the toughest assignments and leave them to sink or swim. Then we wonder why we lose more than 20% of them in their first three years and close to 50% in our urban areas. This brain drain has to stop.

In similar fashion, Columbia University's National Commission on Teaching and America's Future (1996) recommends the following policy changes:

- Increase the ability of financially disadvantaged districts to pay for qualified teachers and insist that school districts hire only qualified teachers.

- Redesign and streamline hiring at the district level, principally by creating a central "electronic hiring hall" for all qualified candidates and establishing cooperative relationships with universities to encourage early hiring of teachers.

- Eliminate barriers to teacher mobility by promoting reciprocal interstate licensing and by working with states to develop portable pensions.

- Provide incentives (including scholarships and premium pay) to recruit teachers for high-need subjects and locations.

- Develop high-quality pathways to teaching for recent graduates, mid-career changers, paraprofessionals already in the classroom, and military and government retirees.

In a more recent statement of the National Commission on Teaching and America's Future (1999), the importance of mentorship programs is stressed:

> Maintaining an adequate supply of well-prepared recruits is even harder during times of substantial new hiring, because new teachers leave at much greater rates than mid-career teachers, particularly if they do not receive mentoring or support during their first years of teaching. Typically, 30 to 50% of beginning teachers leave teaching within the first five years. Teachers in shortage fields, such as the physical sciences, also tend to leave more quickly and at higher rates. New teachers often leave because they are given the most challenging teaching assignments and left to sink or swim with little or no support. The kinds of supervised internships provided for new entrants in other professions—architects, psychologists, nurses, doctors, engineers—are largely absent in

*teaching, even though they have proven to be quite
effective in the few places where they exist.*
(National Commission on Teaching and America's
Future, 1999)

The recruitment of teachers for U.S. public schools has garnered
the attention of a broad range of educators. A number of initiatives are already in place and more are necessary. These are:
improvement of low salary scales, an increase in benefits and
provision for their portability across jurisdictional boundaries,
effective and sustained involvement of colleges and universities, creation of new pathways to teaching careers and exemplary mentoring for novice teachers.

Impact of the Teacher Shortage on Catholic Schools

At the beginning of the previous section on teacher availability,
I described the personnel challenges faced by the principal of a
prestigious Catholic high school. For those in other parts of the
Catholic sector, who have fewer resources, the problem is more
acute. It is especially alarming that schools which serve low-
income families, arguably the most important contribution of
the Catholic educational community to the common good, will
have the fewest incentives to offer.

It is common knowledge that Catholic school teachers earn less
than their counterparts in the public sector. A recent federal
study found that public school teachers earn 25 to 119 percent
more than private school teachers, depending upon the private
subsector, in which Catholic parochial and conservative
Christian are the poorest paying (National Center for Education
Statistics, 1996b). Another federal study (National Center for
Education Statistics, 1996a, p. 70) reported that, on average, in
the 1993-1994 academic year, people with no experience hired
in private schools earned 73% of the salary of their public
school colleagues (with bachelor's degree, $16,200 vs. $21,900;
with master's degree, $17,600 vs. $24,000). For experienced
teachers, the figure was 67% (with master's degree and 20
years experience, $25,200 vs. $37,200; highest step on schedule,
$27,300 vs. $40,500).

Salary is one element of employee compensation. Private
schools fall behind public schools in benefits paid entirely or in

part by their school or district (National Center for Education Statistics, 1996a, p. 75). Eighty-eight percent of public school teachers receive medical benefits vs. 66% private; for dental insurance the figure is 66% public vs. 40% private; for group life insurance, 62% public vs. 40% private); pension contribution (63% public vs. 52% private).

It is not surprising that the annual attrition rate in private schools (10%) is nearly double that of public schools (6%). More alarming are data from the School and Staffing Survey 1993-94 and the Teacher Follow-up Survey 1994-95 reported in *The Condition of Education 1998* (National Center for Education Statistics, 1998, p. 304).   As shown in the following table describing those who have left their teaching position, private schools are losing younger teachers in much higher percentages than their public counterparts.

AGE IN YEARS	PUBLIC	PRIVATE
<25	2.4%	17.1%
25-29	9.9%	12.0%
30-39	6.3%	14.5%
40-49	3.5%	7.7%
50-59	5.4%	4.5%
60-64	31.0%	10.4%
65+	32.4%	24.0%

In light of the higher rate of departure in private schools among young teachers, it is surprising that private school teachers are more satisfied with their jobs than those in public schools. In a recent national survey, teachers were asked about their levels of satisfaction overall. Nearly half of the private school teachers marked high: 47.6%, while the figure among public public-school teachers was 32%. About the same number marked moderate: 34.3% private vs. 34.6% public. Far fewer private-school teachers marked low: 18% private vs.

33.4% public (National Center for Education Statistics, 1997b, p. 12). One explanation for this is found in another federal study. Teachers in private schools were considerably more likely to report that they received a great deal of support from parents for their work—42 percent compared with 12 percent (National Center for Education Statistics, 1997a, p. 6).

Despite higher levels of satisfaction, Catholic-school superintendents are beginning to notice teacher shortages in their home dioceses, evidenced by initial findings of a survey of diocesan superintendents being conducted currently by Clare Helm at NCEA. To date, 27 arch/diocesan leaders from 16 states across the country have responded. Eighty-five percent of the respondents (23 of the 27) reported a teacher shortage. They report that the subject areas most in need are math, science, specialty areas (music, PE, counseling, computers, art), foreign language and early childhood. They also report a dearth of adequately prepared religion teachers. Superintendents attributed the shortage to the salary gap between public and Catholic schools, hiring bonuses in many states, the large number of retirements from public schools, population growth among school-aged children and mandated reduction in public school class size. These phenomena are sparking aggressive recruitment of prospective teachers and raiding of veterans. Superintendents recommend better publication of openings, utilizing the Web and hotlines for prospective candidates and facilitating inter- and intra-diocesan teacher transfers.

Specific recommendations for addressing the personnel crisis will be given below. First, it is important to examine ways in which the Catholic community is now creatively resourcing its schools.

Current Programmatic Initiatives
Creative Resourcing

The Catholic Network of Volunteer Services (1999) lists 87 programs nationwide that provide volunteer teachers to elementary schools and 67 to secondary schools. In most of these programs, elementary and secondary teaching is one of many options for service. In some, like the Alliance for Catholic Education (ACE) that is highlighted as a SPICE 1998 award-winning program, teaching is the unique focus.

Some of the teacher-corps programs are, like ACE, university-based. The Response-ability Program at Rosemont College places teachers in Philadelphia, Washington, San Francisco and Los Angeles. The Urban Catholic Teacher Corps, a joint initiative of Boston College and the Archdiocese of Boston, places trained and certified teachers in local inner-city schools. The Lalanne Program at the University of Dayton offers a similar opportunity for trained and certified teachers. The University of Portland is launching a program. Other institutions, including the University of San Francisco, Loyola-Marymount University, the College of St. Rose and the University of Dallas, are in the planning stages. This year the University of Notre Dame began an initiative through which Catholic colleges and universities can share information and expertise about teacher-corps initiatives.

Some teacher-corps programs are statewide, as in Texas and Florida. Others have operated within a diocesan framework, as in New York, Washington, Los Angeles and Seattle. In Chicago the Inner City Teaching Corps, an independent organization operating in conjunction with the archdiocese, places volunteers in elementary schools. Some programs are parish-based, such as Our Lady of the Lake Catholic School in Arkansas or parishes serving Native American communities such as St. Francis and St. Bonaventure in New Mexico.

Other programs, most of them associated with a religious community, are school based. Recent college graduates, mostly without professional training, apprentice under master teachers and live together in community. Examples include Mother Caroline Academy in Boston, run by the School Sisters of Notre Dame; Bishop Perry Middle School in New Orleans, run by the Edmundite Fathers; Nativity Preparatory School in Milwaukee, a SPICE 1997 award-winner run by the Jesuits, along with sister Jesuit schools in New York, Boston, Omaha, Baltimore and Detroit; and Seton Academy in Baltimore, run by a consortium of religious communities. There are now 24 such institutions nationwide, and many more are in the planning stages (Anderson, 1999, p. 16).

According to the Catholic Network of Volunteer Services (1999), religious communities sponsor volunteer corps that place young people in a wide variety of settings. While these do not have the specific educational focus of the organizations already mentioned, they include elementary and secondary teaching as options. Among the religious communities whose volunteer programs include teaching are Adorers of the Precious Blood, Congregation of Notre Dame, Religious of the Assumption, Missionary Sisters of the Sacred Heart of Jesus, Capucin Franciscan Friars, Carmelites, Claretians, Vincentians, Dominicans, Sisters of St. Francis, Franciscan Friars, Congregation of the Holy Cross, Christian Brothers, Marists, Marianists, Sisters of Mercy, Brothers of the Sacred Heart, Benedictines, Piarists, Sisters of Divine Providence, Religious of Jesus and Mary, Sisters of Providence, Salesians, Sisters of Charity, Ursulines, Sisters of St. Joseph, Servants of the Immaculate Heart and the Society of Jesus.

Most of the current programmatic initiatives for creative staffing of schools are in their infancy. Many Catholic educators, independent of each other, have tapped into the intelligence, generosity and faith commitment of young Catholics. It is interesting to note that religious communities, which for many years virtually dominated Catholic schools in the United States, are giving birth to a new generation of lay people in schools. Some elements of religious life remain, such as voluntary poverty, community life and built-in mentorship. However, creative new lay structures and charisms are being born in these organizations.

Creative Resourcing in the Future

Programmatic initiatives for creative staffing of schools alone cannot solve the impending teacher shortage. Catholic educators must pay attention to issues of remuneration, the role of the higher-education sector and the role of national organizations.

Catholic schools simply must offer higher salaries and greater benefits if they are to attract qualified teachers. At one time, the Catholic community resourced its schools through human capital, members of religious orders who gave a lifetime of *pro bono* service. The dramatic decline of vocations to religious life in the United States eliminated this solution. Now the Catholic community must contribute financial resources to compete in the marketplace of teachers. In a highly mobile society, the church should also create mechanisms for portability of salary level and benefits across geographic and sectoral (private, diocesan and parochial) boundaries.

Catholic colleges and universities must have more sustained involvement in the preparation and retention of teachers in Catholic schools. At present, initial indicators are that little is being done systematically. In a forthcoming report in the journal *Catholic Education: A Journal of Inquiry and Practice*, Sr. Mary Peter Traviss will present some initial findings from a survey of Catholic colleges and universities that have teacher-training programs. Very few institutions offer programs specifically geared to Catholic schools. More disturbing is the fact that a large number of people in teacher-education programs report that they feel no special responsibility for staffing Catholic schools. It is unfortunate that, as private institutions, Catholic colleges and universities charge exorbitant tuition and fees. Many students graduate in significant debt and literally cannot afford to teach in a Catholic school. Catholic colleges and universities must work with local schools and dioceses to offer special financial-aid incentives, such as grants and loan forgiveness. Conversely, dioceses and schools must appreciate the serious fiscal constraints under which higher education works. Moreover, they should be willing to partner with higher education in its mission of research and teacher preparation.

National Catholic organizations, such as the National Catholic Educational Association, the United States Catholic Conference and FADICA, can act as coordinating mechanisms for dioceses, religious orders, higher education institutions and private schools. They can identify exemplary programs like ACE and make them available for replication nationwide. They can develop models of portability of benefits across sectors. Based on some of the public-school organizations mentioned in the first section of the chapter, they can sponsor job clearinghouses via the Web, hotlines and publications. They can sponsor research on staffing issues. Lastly, the national organizations could organize a symposium that would help the Catholic community reflect on the impending teacher shortage and devise appropriate responses.

References

Anderson, G. "Small Middle Schools on the Rise." *America* 180 (1999): 18, 16-18.

Archer, J. "States Anteing Up Supplements to Teachers Certified by Board." *Education Week* 18, no 12 (November 18, 1998): 1, 12.

Bradley, A. "New Teachers Are Hot Commodity." *Education Week* 18, no. 1 (1998): 1, 20.

Response: Volunteer Opportunity Directory 1999 (1999). Washington, DC: Catholic Network of Volunteer Services. Retrieved June 1999 from the World Wide Web: http://www.cnvs.org.

Draper, N. "Teachers Who Call It Quits Cause Shortage Concern." *Minneapolis Star Tribune* (March 10, 1999): 1B.

Feistritzer, C. Emily. "Alternative Teacher Certification—An Overview." Washington, D.C.: National Center for Education Information (February 1998). Retrieved June 1999 from the World Wide Web: http://www.ncei.com/Alt-Teacher-Cert.htm.

————. "The Truth Behind the 'Teacher Shortage.'" *The Wall Street Journal* (January 28, 1998).

National Center for Education Statistics. *America's Teachers: Profile of a Profession 1993-1994.* Washington, D.C.: United States Department of Education (1996a).

————. *America's Teachers: Profile of a Profession.* Washington, D.C.: United States Department of Education (1997c).

————. *The Condition of Education 1998.* Washington, D.C.: United States Department of Education (1998).

————. *The Condition of Education 1997.* Washington, D.C.: United States Department of Education (1997a).

————. *Job Satisfaction Among America's Teachers: Effects of Workplace Conditions, Background Characteristics, and Teacher Compensation.* Washington, D.C.: United States Department of Education (1997b).

————. *The Patterns of Teacher Compensation.* Washington, D.C.: United States Department of Education (1996b).

National Commission on Teaching and America's Future. *Briefing Paper: Recruiting Teachers.* New York: Teachers College (1999). Retrieved June 1999 from the World Wide Web: http://www.tc.columbia.edu/~teach comm/brief0.htm.

————. *What Matters Most: Teaching for America's Future.* New York: Teachers College (1996).

National Education Association. "A Qualified Teacher in Every Classroom." Washington, DC (1999). Retrieved June 1999 from the World Wide Web: http://www.nea.org/qps/qtc.htm.

Recruiting New Teachers, Inc. "Teacher Shortages in America" (1999). Retrieved June 1999 from the World Wide Web: http://www.rnt.org.

Riley, Richard W. "New Challenges, A New Resolve: Moving American Education into the 21st Century" (February 16, 1999). Retrieved June 1999 from the World Wide Web: http://www.ed.gov/Speeches/02-1999/990216.html.

United States Department of Education. Web site on Higher Education Amendments of 1998 (1999). Retrieved June 1999 from the World Wide Web: http://www.ed.gov.

Chapter 8

The Board's Role in Financing and Resourcing Catholic Schools

– Lee Brennan, Lawrence S. Callahan, Regina M. Haney

This publication presents many ideas to finance and resource Catholic schools. An idea remains only an idea until someone or some group takes the necessary steps to make it a reality.

The SPICE programs presented at the Conversations in Excellence symposium and pre-sented again in this book are excellent ideas that, if adapted, would impact positively the school's finances.

School and diocesan boards, commissions or coun-cils can assist the administration to implement these ideas. Finances, including development and third-source funding, are identified as one of the responsibilities of Catholic education governing groups. This is supported by recent survey research conducted by Convey and Haney.[1] The research further states that effective boards have achievement in the areas of development/fundraising, budget/financial stability, long-range planning, marketing/public relations/recruitment and plant upgrade (p. 44).

This chapter will discuss three aspects of the board's contribution to the financial health of the school. These are:

1. Importance of boards and what makes them work
2. Financial management testing the budget and plan
3. Allocation of financial assistance

Why are boards important and what makes them work? To answer these questions, let's turn to the National Association of Boards of Catholic Education (NABE) outstanding board awardees. Each year, NABE recognizes boards that have made a significant difference in the institution that they govern. The following are two examples of the board's impact on schools.

• A school in financial distress and under serious consideration for closing was saved due to the board's development of a long-range strategic plan and a five-year facilities plan. The board raised the money to construct a 10,000 square-foot gymnasium/cafeteria and to renovate the former cafeteria into classrooms to accommodate current growth. The board implemented a development program and annual fund campaign. The board members researched, planned and implemented the compensation efforts to recruit and retain professional staff, resulting in a competitive salary and benefits package. As a result of board actions, the school is financially strong and stable.

• A school blessed with a strong budget and dedicated board members has created a "case statement" that provides compelling reasons why anyone should consider investing time, talents and treasures in support of or to advance the cause of the school. The case statement is a well-defined and refined vision of the school's future. The board members are strong communicators. They use a *Parent Pack* weekly newsletter and a "state of the school" yearly meeting to reach parents and the parish community. These board members listened to the community last year by holding two constituency meetings with a total attendance of over 300. Because of what they heard at these meetings, they developed task forces to address issues such as facilities, enrollment, development, finances, volunteerism and curriculum.

The mission of the school drives the work of the board. The board's commitment to the mission touches all the responsibilities of the board. The responsibilities are:

- Policy
- Curriculum
- Quality education
- Facilities
- Planning
- Development, public relations, marketing
- Finances

It is the mission that drives the decisions of the board. For example, in order to ensure "quality, Catholic education" the board assists the administration to develop and finance a three-year technology plan. To support the element of the mission, "educate the whole person," the board sets a policy that requires all students to participate in the religious education program. It is the board members' commitment to mission, "gospel-centered education within a faith community," that compels them to articulate and promote it to the public.

In order to take the mission phrase, "develop disciple-citizens," off the page and to see it lived out, board members first educate themselves about the meaning of the phrase. Faculty members provided 15-minute inservice sessions for the board at the beginning of several meetings. The board models the mission in its decisions about tuition assistance and admissions. The school opens its doors to those who desire a Catholic education and who can not pay full tuition.

The board realizes the mission when each member solicits donors to support the $100,000 renovation of the science lab in order to "sustain an environment in which students are encouraged to question and to discover knowledge." Decisions, actions and policies of the board must reflect the mission—an important role for boards.

The board's role in finances enables it to move the mission from a plan to reality, providing the best Catholic education for those whom the school serves. What fuels the work of the board and ultimately the mission is the school's finances.

To put the school on a sound financial footing the board has the responsibility to do two things:

1. Assume financial responsibility for the institution, which includes the budget, audits and investments.
2. Provide leadership in fund raising and developing third-source funding.

Board research conducted by NABE supports the role of boards in finance. Grade "A" or effective boards are likely to be more involved than other boards with issues pertaining to budget and planning. In terms of accomplishments, grade "A" boards are more likely than other boards to list development/fund raising and budget/financial stability as their achievements. For example, one board was able to implement its decision to offer financial assistance to families who wish to send their children to a Catholic school because it designed a way to obtain the funds. Finances provided the fuel that made this idea a reality.

We know from our service on boards or committees that if we obtain funding for a project, as well as plan it, the time put into the project is worthwhile. The success gives influence and power to the group. The group is effective because it makes things happen. As the Nike ad says, "Just do it!" If boards raise the money through budgets, fund raising, development or connections, they too, "just do it."

The board's financial skill touches all the work of the board. It impacts the board's policy decisions. To provide equitable staff salaries and benefit packages requires dollars. To formulate and implement an affordable tuition policy requires the finances to back it up.

The board's aptitude for finances touches curriculum. To keep in step with today's education, the board must find the "big bucks" to support the school's technology plan. If the school integrates technology into the teaching and learning, it must have the necessary hardware and software as well as trained staff.

The board's competency in the financial arena influences the quality of the school because it enables the school to have arts programs, access to the Internet, a state-of-the-art library, tuition money for teachers to attend classes and workshops, etc.

The board's financial expertise sways positively the decisions regarding maintenance and renovations of the facilities. With the board's competent financial leadership, the school community continually is able to look ahead and plan to address future needs of the institution. It is the board's role to see that the priorities identified in the technology plan are complete, and that a plan to fund them is in place.

In the area of third-source funding, development, marketing and public relations, the board shapes, approves, articulates and serves as advocate for these areas. It is the board that moves dreams to reality by its willingness to recognize an institution's needs and sense of purpose.

In addition to financial expertise, personal wealth should also determine who sits around the board table. A colleague who worked North Carolina believed that board members should, "give, get or get off." The ability to give or identify those who can give should be an important criterion for membership on the board because finances touch all aspects of the board's work and impact the board's effectiveness.

In the NCEA publication *Dollars and Sense*, Michael Guerra reports that 50 percent of all Catholic high school boards are expected to donate to the school, while 75 percent of private school boards are expected to do so.

The *golden rule* means that those with the gold RULE! Applied to the role of boards, board members who have their eyes focused on the institution's mission and who assume financial responsibility and leadership for funding the mission make a difference!

Testing the Budget and Plan

Now that the board member has responsibility for the gold, how does he/she handle it responsibly? Lee Brennan, board member in the Diocese of Trenton, presents this advice:

> *With the advent of spreadsheet programs such as Lotus 123 and Excel, the ability to prepare well-formatted and arithmetically precise budgets is available to most schools and school advisory boards. Thanks to user-friendly word processing and graphics programs, the same can be said for preparing planning documents. However, if the two tasks, i.e. planning and budgeting, are not performed in concert with one another, it is unlikely that their usefulness and relevance will be greatly enhanced by the hitech tools.*

It is well understood that achievement of any major goal or plan must be accomplished in steps. It also is a fact that almost all goals and visions will require funding to become a reality. Thus, in achieving a school's vision and plan, the annual budget serves as the road map and provides details of the steps necessary to test that vision on a regular basis against the reality of the budget process. Conversely, the preparation of the budget always should begin with an objective review of how well the school is moving towards its stated goals.

A sample outline is the following:

Vision Statement
- State the vision and long term direction.

Goal and Objective
- State the desired goal.
- State the desired objective.

How do we get there?
- Review relevant historical information.
- Review original assumptions that are no longer valid.
- Identify structural changes.

Build the program

- Analyze where you are.

- Identify changes needed to:
  - improve progress,
  - adjust to enrollment changes.

- Adjust to policy changes.

- Identify all personnel needs.

- Test against your plan/vision.

- Cost out the program.

- Attempt to fund it.

- Prioritize changes and run it again.

This process of annually testing the plan against the budget and the budget against the plan should not necessarily result in changing the school's goals, but it will likely result in some changes in the path taken to achieve the goals.

The following are tips that Mr. Brennan provides so that boards will lead with the Midas touch—turning the budget process into gold—that is, golden opportunities to be a financially healthy school:

- Plan for the future. Changes will come in enrollment, technology, salary and benefits. It is easier to get where you want to in steps rather than leaps.

- Have a three-year salary scale for the faculty and update it as it expires.

- Establish a development committee and endowment fund now.

- Look at enrollment trends each September when there is an actual head count.

- Have a standing finance committee with financial expertise.

- Have a diversified board with expertise in finance, facility management and PTA liaison.

- Prepare an annual budget based on actual historical performance and a program-by-program evaluation of changes.

- Make sure your schedule fits into the budget schedule of your parish or funding source.
- Have input from all parties (principal, pastor, PTA) on all budget issues.
- Track actual performance monthly, and focus on variations from the budget. Implement corrective actions as soon as possible.

The Advantages of a Third-Party Service in Allocating Financial Assistance

A challenging board responsibility is to keep tuition affordable. Lawrence Callahan, superintendent of Catholic schools for the Archdiocese of Washington, D.C., presents negotiated tuition, based on a family's ability to pay, as one creative response to making tuition affordable. According to Mr. Callahan, there are four possible ways to determine what a family can afford to pay.

One is negotiated tuition, which was initiated in his diocese a number of years ago. In this model, each family sits down individually with the pastor and the principal, who ask, "How much of the $1,500 tuition for your child can you afford to pay?" The parent might say, "I think I can pay $1,000." Then an agreed-upon amount must be negotiated. This takes an enormous commitment of time, and on that basis, we don't recommend it. It's almost impossible to sit down with every parent unless you have a very small school, and even then time is a critical factor.

The second is the pastor/principal application review. In this process, each family completes an application. The pastor and principal review the application and try to determine individual family need—for one family, perhaps $100, for others $200 or $300. This also requires an enormous commitment of time, complicated further by what formula to use, especially when there are many factors to look at on each application. We don't recommend this approach either.

The third is a Tuition Assistance Committee. The pastor or principal establishes a committee within the parish to review applications. The draw-back to this method is that parents do not want information about their financial condition made public.

And there is no guarantee of confidentiality, since it is human nature to talk.

The fourth option for determining the amount of tuition a family can afford is through a third-party service. We think the third-party service is the best alternative for everyone. We recommended this approach to all parishes and schools in Baltimore, as far back as 1989. This service develops the application. It provides formulas to determine need. Confidentiality is guaranteed. The parent sends the application to the firm; no one else sees it. We would suggest that over the next ten years, every diocese is going to move to using third-party service. It saves you resources and time; a service has all the elements to be successful. Our experience is that it is the best option, but you should always do what's best for you.

What are the elements of an application? What do you have to look for if you decide to develop your own application? First, you need family information, for example, whether it is a one or two parent household, the number of dependents, and whether there are foster children. You also need to know the family's expenses. What tuition are they paying? Do they have children in college? These are valid expenses that help to determine a family's actual need.

You also need information on income. What are the salaries of the family members? Do they have income-producing rentals? Do they receive interest from investments? Do they have assets such as a second home? All of this information must be built into a formula in order to make decisions.

What criteria will you need in order to award grants in a just way to a school or diocese or parish? Every parish, whether it has a school or not, should be providing tuition assistance, supporting all those who believe in Catholic education. The local archbishop or bishop should make certain that everyone understands the importance of contributing to the Catholic education ministry. In addition, you need to decide if you want to give tuition assistance to non-parishioners or just limit it to parishioners. Do you want to give it to Catholics only or do you want to give it to everyone? Many people want to give to everyone, but there are some parishes and schools that say,

"Wait a minute, this money was generated through the parish, and I'd like to give it to Catholics." You have to make that decision.

You also have to determine the timeline for the application process. When will applications be submitted? When will they be reviewed? When will you tell people if they are receiving a grant? They need to know in order to make a decision about coming to your school.

You have to determine how much money is available to be allocated. Do you have $60,000? More? Less?

As far as allocation is concerned, you have to determine the percentage of assistance to individual families. Do you want to provide assistant once to meet their full need? Or do you want to meet 50 percent of need? We never recommend that you pay the full amount, because there should be a commitment on the family's part, as well, to make a sacrifice.

So, how much will a family receive? You may have only $60,000 available. You will have to pool everyone involved in the application process and allocate based on two considerations: what you have available and family needs. It is a good process, but it requires a complicated formula. That's why we recommend that you use professionals.

Will the third-party service pool your money and allocate it across the population? If you give them a number that is available, say $60,000 or $80,000, they will generate the amount of the grant and spread it across the pool of applicants based on family need, much like college assistance programs. Many high schools are now doing this. In addition, if you say, "I'd like to hold $10,000 back for emergencies," they will take whatever you have available and hold back $10,000 for needs that come up in late applications. For example, a parent may develop a serious illness and unexpectedly need tuition assistance. We always recommend you hold back some money for this kind of emergency and ask the third-party service to process any late application due to special circumstances.

How are third-party services paid? The parent completes the application and sends a fee of $13 or $14 with the application.

That pays for the whole process. The parish also pays a very small fee, perhaps $75-$90 annually.

Will you please describe the third-party process? Each family receives instructions and information for each section of the application and, by the way, these are available in Spanish and English. The information is very thorough and the instruction sheet answers any questions. There also is a toll-free number. If parents have a question, they don't have to burden the school. They call the provider directly. Does that mean that you do not need to have somebody at the school helping people with this? Definitely not, although there should be a liaison, for instance, a school secretary, who distributes forms.

Conclusion

As the board embraces and exercises its financial leadership, it may decide to adapt one or more of the 1998 SPICE programs.

This chapter is adapted from an article in *Issue-Gram*, the newsletter of the National Association of Boards of Catholic Education, NCEA, Washington, DC, Vol. 7, No. 1 (Spring 1997).

Endnote

[1]   John Convey and Regina Haney, *Benchmarks in Excellence* (Washington, DC: National Catholic Educational Association, 1997).

Chapter 9

The Spirituality of Leadership

– Howard Gray, SJ

In a helpful essay on administration as ministry
(1986), Charles Beirne, a Jesuit educator with
experience in both North and Central America as
well as in secondary and university education, suggests two models for administrators: John the
Baptist, "the prophet who prepares the way of
the Lord" or Peter, "the spontaneous ex-fisherman
trying to help advance the Kingdom, but who
rather constantly puts his foot in his mouth."

These images, and many more, do fit the role at
times. Administrators, like the models in
Scriptures, have to admit personal weaknesses,
reflect on experience and keep discovering the

nature of their calling by the Lord. Like other forms of ministry, administration implies service to the community, a way of responding to a call of the Lord. Through institutions like high schools and universities, one serves within the church but for the world (Beirne, 1986, pp. 1-2). He lays out the wide designs that describe administrators' roles in a Christian school system.

I want to add two elements, featured in the title of this morning's talk: (l) the greatest service of administrators is to lead and (2) the direction of that leadership is toward mission. In phrases like these: "prepares the way of the Lord," "to help advance the Kingdom," "serves the church for the world," Beirne indicates what that mission could involve. Radically, the defining mission in the Catholic enterprise is to sustain and to further the Reign of God preached, taught and exemplified by Jesus and donated through the Spirit to the church.

That enterprise—the mission of Christ entrusted to the church—demands the Spirit's attentive presence. Leadership needs a spirituality, a reflective way to guide decisions and to evaluate their Christian effectiveness. To get at this, I want to unpack two heavy-laden items, "spirituality" and "leadership." *Spirituality*, as I define it, is the way women and men journey to God, that allegory signifying the human pilgrimage through mystery to Ultimate Mystery.

There are many maps which Christian brothers and sisters have drawn to walk that pilgrimage: Mercy, Dominican, Franciscan, monastic and lay, feminine and masculine. But, ultimately, each of these maps is a variant on the One who is the way—the Christ who showed the way. Today, "spirituality" has become a diffuse and burdensome term symbolizing a variety of philosophies, techniques and strategies. It embraces a horde of interests from sports to sexual preferences to ethnic origins to business ventures to the control of addictive behavior to the color of crystals. To complicate the scene, cherished Christian symbols—the Cross, stained-glass windows of saints, rosaries, Gregorian chant and angels—have been adopted as jewelry, home furniture, cafe fixtures and cutesy magnets riveted to refrigerator doors reminding all that the Little League game starts at 6:00 p.m. in Kiwanis Park.

Thus, contemporary notions of spirituality are weighed down by a mass of adaptations, misappropriations and usurpation of images, symbols and rituals—all remote from the tough simplicity of the pilgrimage to God in the likeness of Christ. Nonetheless, it is this pure definition of spirituality that governs what I mean here. What I would add is the distinction between a tourist and a pilgrim. Our temptation is to become tourists—to collect souvenirs, to hurry along to make the next destination, to take pictures, to try to find a McDonald's in an otherwise foreign environment. No, we have to be pilgrims—to become better viewers, more contemplative, to establish partnerships with our fellow pilgrims, to find in the Eucharist the food and drink that keeps us moving along, impatient, only to find the Kingdom.

The second term, *leadership*, is similarly burdened by conflicting descriptions, slick reductionisms, too-clever techniques, and pseudo-religious language like "transformation for lasting success," or "making profits self-actualizing," or "the Gospel is good business." Borrowing shamelessly from Howard Gardner (1995), I would call leadership an empowerment for influencing people toward ways of thinking, ways of action, ways of renewing a tradition. Adapting his generic description to Christian leadership, I mean the power of the example of the historical Jesus to influence people for the Kingdom and the power of his Spirit to sustain that mission.

Spirituality and leadership are the power to influence others to accept, to enrich, to act for the sake of the Kingdom or Reign of God as they journey through life. My remarks fall under two major headings: 1) the process of Christian spirituality which supports and evaluates that structure of leadership and 2) the structure of Christian leadership itself. Finally, I shall connect this all to the topic of this symposium: "Creatively Financing and Resourcing Catholic Schools."

Structure of Christian Leadership. Jesus' teaching mission incorporates four actions: he teaches people how to see; he teaches people how to feel; he teaches people how to confront evil, especially public, structured evil and he teaches people how to move beyond enmity to solidarity, into a community of reconciliation. Let me give an example:

Now, Jesus was teaching in one of the synagogues on the Sabbath. And there was a woman who had an infirmity for eighteen years. She was bent over and could not fully straighten herself. And when Jesus saw her, he called her and said to her, "Woman, you are freed from your infirmity." And he laid his hands upon her, and immediately, she was made straight, and she praised God. But the ruler of the synagogue, indignant because Jesus had healed on the Sabbath, said to the people, "There are six days on which work ought to be done; come on those days and be healed, and not on the Sabbath day." Then, the Lord answered him, "You hypocrite! Does not each of you on the Sabbath untie his ox or his ass from the manger, and head it away to water it? And ought not this woman, a daughter of Abraham who Satan found for eighteen years, be loosed from this bond on the Sabbath day?" As he said this, all his adversaries were put to shame; and all the people rejoiced at all the glorious things that were done by him. (Luke 13:10–17)

Note the sequence—Jesus sees evil, from his later explanation clearly feels evil, then confronts evil on two levels (action and interpretation) and creates a new community of liberation.

Christian leadership does not simply find proof-texts and give homiletic inspiration, it also finds a method and acts for its mission. Simply and directly put, Christian educational leadership goes beyond academic and professional excellence. The "beyond" leads people to be attentive, to learn how to see, to have hearts ready to respond to need, to be courageous enough to name what dehumanizes and enslaves, and to help form a common ground of reconciliation where oppressors and oppressed, victims and tyrants, strong and weak can learn how to live along side one another.

Frequently, I am asked, "How?" "How do you help faculty, students, parents and board members see and respond to this Christian structure?" I agree with Gardner that what every leader has is a story, an audience, an organization, the chance to embody what you need to accomplish, direct and indirect ways to present this, and the exposure to give credibility to your vision.

In Catholic organizations, be they the diocese, the school, the parish or the religious community, our story is the gospel and the embarrassing richness of commentary to enliven the meaning of that gospel. Our audience is a constituency that has chosen to be there, some because they have no place else to go. Our task is to embody that gospel in the difficult choices and often overwhelming tasks of administration. How, for example, does our gospel-based spirituality affect our fiscal priorities, our decisions on hiring and promoting personnel, our support of colleagues and those under our care, our ability to delegate to others? How do we balance our spiritual gifts with our professional and native ability? The structures of seeing, feeling, confronting and reconciling are elements of Christian mission. The more leaders live with their priorities, the more they find their potential.

To "see" in the light of God, one must develop a contemplative habit, the time to dwell with reality. Prayer, walking, reading poetry, gardening, music, journaling, whatever. One needs "Sabbath Sight" to "feel" in the light of God. One needs time to develop care, memories and understanding in order to confront fear, biases and prejudices. Maybe an occasional explicit service to others is called for. One needs conversation to touch the Christian imagination. The role of imagination is key if one is to feel. Lawrence Thornton (1987, p. 65) articulates it well:

> They see sheep and terrorists because they image us that way. But look at the people, Silvio, that old woman, the man in shirt sleeves. They remember a time before the regime, but they do not take their imaginations beyond memory because hoping is too painful. So long as we accept what the men in the car imagine, we're finished. All I've been trying to tell you is that there are two Argentinas, Silvio, the regime's travesty of it, and the one we have in our hearts...We have to believe in the power of imagination because it is all we have, and ours is stronger than theirs.

To feel and to voice indignation is another central element in the spirituality of leadership. I don't know of any area of spiritual life that we ignore more than indignation. I do not mean political pique because I lose or I don't like a particular politician or I am fed up with mediocre sports teams. I mean attention to reality, taking time to see and to voice my care, sharing my values with those I trust, uncovering moral and religious evil. Recently, I led a discussion among younger staff personnel. One member, discussing a case study, dismissed "Catholic guilt." I called him on this—What do you mean by that? Vague complaints centered on sexual instructions. I asked them about the slum landlord, the male who date rapes, someone who cheats people—everything is all right as long as no one feels bad about it.

Cultivated spiritual discontent and well-argued prophetic protest are Christian. While too frequently the neurotic and chronically unhappy employ protest as therapy, the deeper redemption of Christian public confrontation has a place in our spiritual life. Christians are supposed to mourn and to be indignant about injustice, victimization and tyranny.

Finally, we live in reconciliation. Not a wishy-washy, vague tolerance, e.g., "Don't shake my tree and I won't shake yours," but a Christian ability to see a greater common good, to work for it, even with people I may not want to vacation with, because this is what Christ finally does. Forgiveness leads to communion.

Conclusion

You have come to dig into how to uncover, to develop and to reorient resources to keep Catholic education vital and influential, able to do its immediate job of educating youth but also its political job of voicing alternatives to secularized education. The goal of this presentation is simply to remind you of how we are different and of how we can cultivate a graced plurality. But let me end by illustrating the importance of resources.

Some years ago, I worked among Cambodian refugees, over 100,000 of them, who were gathered at the Thai-Cambodian refuge. Remember that these refugees made it to freedom because they knew how to lie, steal, barter and, sometimes, kill in order to achieve freedom for themselves and their families. When they came to the camp, Site II, they did not change. They continued to want to achieve the final freedom of life in the First World. One of these refugees was nothing like this.

He was a dignified, self-contained individual, a man of talent and moral concern. Near the end of my stay, he asked me to come to his home and to meet his family at a dinner. When that day came, I accompanied him to his home. On the way I asked him, "Sambath, what is it that you want most out of life?" He replied, "Oh, Father, I want to be a good man. I want to teach my children not to hate. I want them to live in trust. That is why I want them to meet you, my friend. They have never met a Caucasian before who was not in authority. I want them to meet you as my new friend."

I could not approach the integrity that Buddhist gentleman exhibited. He taught me so much about God's work in all peoples and in all religions. I determined that when I had the chance, I would do all that I could to help him and his family to reach freedom and security in the USA. I could do nothing by myself, but through the good officers of the Jesuit school system and their willingness to sponsor him and his family, I was able to arrange for this man to come to the USA where he has begun to achieve his dream. So, today, when we speak about resources as an essential ingredient to our education, think of this episode. No good is accomplished without resources. No Kingdom, even that of God, can be fulfilled without human cooperation. This is why your programs and your reflections are so important.

References

Beirne, C. "Compass and catalyst: An essay on the ministry of administration." *Studies in the Spirituality of Jesuits*. 18(2), 1986.

Gardner, H. *Leading minds: An anatomy of leadership*. New York: Basic Books, 1995.

Thornton, L. *Imagining Argentina*. New York: Doubleday, 1987.

Chapter 10

Points of View: Perspectives from Diocesan Leaders

– Robert R. Bimonte, FSC; Timothy W. Dwyer; Daniel J. Elsener;
Jerome Porath; Ann Dominic Roach, OP;
Lourdes Sheehan, RSM; Michael Skube

Several years ago at a gathering to recognize a university staff member's contributions, I heard the president of the university state something that made me appreciate more the importance of college-level education. The president said that, "A university must be a place where rich conversations are conducted. If stimulating exchange of thoughts, opinions and feelings do not take place, then the university has no reason to exist."

Based on this rationale, I'm proud that the SPICE program, a collaborative effort with a university, Boston College, annually brings scholars, researchers and practitioners around the table to engage in *Conversations in Excellence,* a rich dialogue on the topic of Catholic education. The previous chapters capture the many thoughts, opinions and feelings that were expressed during the many rich conversations over the four-day program. This final chapter mirrors for the participants, through a panel of superintendents, the themes and trends that emerged as they discussed creative ways to finance and resource Catholic schools.

Six superintendents and the CACE (Chief Administrators of Catholic Education) executive director were invited to serve on the panel. Brother Robert Bimonte, FSC, panel facilitator, asked them to come not only to participate but also to listen. After all, someone once said, "Silence is one great art of conversation." They identified these themes: leadership, alternative development models, redesigning Catholic education to accomplish more with less, basic assumptions about Catholic schools' stewardship of financial gifts and issues surrounding vouchers. What follows are six questions which the panel shaped around these themes. One panelist responded to each question.

—Regina Haney

Question One

Realizing that the world of Catholic education has definitely changed, what are the implications for the selection, formation and ongoing professional development of leaders?

Respondent: Mr. Timothy Dwyer, superintendent of schools, Diocese of Rochester, New York

The demands on leaders in Catholic education are increasing in number and intensity. Financial support for schools continues to transfer from parishes to parents. An increasing number of Catholic educators have themselves not enjoyed the benefits of a Catholic education. As a result, we look to the principal (at the local level) and the superintendent (at the diocesan level) to carry the torch and continue the rich tradition of Catholic schools.

Recent publications provide wonderful guidance for principals regarding their critical role as spiritual, managerial and educational leader of the school. In many ways, the superintendent assumes similar roles in her/his dealings with principals. Catholic school leaders need, however, to know more than how to lead their own circle of influence. The changing landscape requires that leaders must be aware of and active in the bigger picture, namely, the diocesan, state and national trends and events that affect Catholic education. Principals familiar with the state of the schools in their diocese and aware of the challenges and achievements of their neighboring schools, have a richer perspective and can more effectively administer their own school. Likewise, superintendents who are active in the NCEA, who meet with their regional counterparts and who participate in national initiatives, leverage their influence in a much more productive way.

More than ever before, Catholic schools must see themselves as interdependent and involved in a ministry whose collective value far exceeds the sum of its individual parts. The most successful schools in the future will be those that effectively share resources in ever-widening circles. This can only happen through an understanding that, no matter what our ministry, we are part of a bigger picture in which every effective leader must simultaneously be an effective and contributing follower.

I would strongly encourage every Catholic school leader to expand their circle of concern and become active at a level beyond their current circle of influence. This participation will energize and inform. It will pay rich dividends in the effectiveness of "routine" duties.

Question Two
Traditionally, our approach to development has been one school at a time, everyone fending for him/herself. Are there alternative models we need to explore?

Respondent: Dr. Michael Skube, superintendent of schools, Diocese of Charlotte, North Carolina
Alternative models can be approached on a diocesan or regional level or both. On a diocesan level the structure or framework to involve people could be a diocesan foundation. Representatives would be from various parts of the diocese. On a regional level the foundation would be for the schools within the geographically-designated area and, ideally, each school would have a representative on the board.

The overall responsibilities of the regional foundation could be the following areas:

1. cultivation of public relations;
2. sponsorship of special events;
3. management of an annual fund drive;
4. implementation of capital campaigns;
5. establishment of memorial programs;
6. operation of coordinated planned giving programs including wills, bequests, life insurance, etc.; and
7. establishment of an alumni association.

A full–time development director would be employed to work with the schools and the foundation.

All of these areas would be approached in a coordinated way as in the following suggestions:

- A brochure highlighting the regional schools could be distributed to realtors. These brochures would reach a wider audience and be cost-effective than those geared to individual schools. Inexpensive fact sheets could also be developed and annually updated by each school.

- Parent Teacher Organizations would continue to sponsor special events for their own individual schools but one special event, such as an auction could be sponsored annually be each PTO with the proceeds split among the regional schools for specific projects, for example, a tuition assistance fund.

- One annual fund could be sponsored for the area schools with people given the option of designating funds for a particular school.

- Capital campaigns, another cost-effective measure, could be sponsored for all schools and run as one which would illustrate common directives of the schools.

- The same could be applied to memorial, planned giving and alumni programs.

Question Three

We all know the importance of having a common vision. What is the basic assumption we need to identify as to why we support Catholic schools?

Respondent: Mr. Daniel J. Elsener, Archdiocese of Indianapolis, Indiana

The basic assumption is that properly formed and educated youth benefit the individual, local community, church and nation. Therefore, all have a stake in and responsibility to financially support education.

Catholic schools, like all schools that are designed to help families promote the common good and to serve all stratum of society, must be supported by the larger community. Parents alone will not be able to carry the full responsibility of funding education. The degree to which parents are expected to pay the cost should be related to the resources available to the family. Therefore, the cost that cannot be met should be paid by the larger community.

The government, "we the people," pay to support the education of children and not a school system. Moreover, we pay taxes and give donations to education because parents need support in assuming their responsibilities to educate their children. We do not pay taxes because a system needs support.

In summary:
1. All benefit from an educated populace.
2. Because all benefit, all should pay.
3. It is not feasible for most parents to pay the entire cost of educating their youth.

Question Four

Assuming that at some point all of us will be the beneficiary of some financial gift or endowment, what are our responsibilities as stewards of the financial gifts we receive?

Respondent: Sister Ann Dominic Roach, OP, superintendent of schools, Archdiocese of Boston, Massachusetts

As we stand on the brink of the new millennium, Jubilee 2000, the concept of stewardship and our responsibilities as stewards of God's creation is very real. Christian stewardship is the recognition of God's gift of creation and is a personal response of gratitude to God. Our response is expressed in terms of worthy management and care of all resources available for the sustenance and enrichment of life. Stewardship simply put is service to God and His people. Isn't that what we are about as Catholic educators?

The challenge for all of us in Catholic education is to rededicate ourselves to those goals that support the youth in our schools and will shape their future.

As we approach the new millennium, we recognize that Catholic schools are indispensable to the educational mission of the Church and that our schools must maintain their Catholicity and continue sound quality education and formation programs.

Third party funding is a reality if our good work is to continue and prosper. Whether it be endowment, grant money, or tuition assistance programs, all require a fiduciary responsibility. Accountability regarding the just distribution of all gifts is incumbent upon each of us. In my own diocese, the Catholic Schools Foundation, through an annual dinner and the cultivation of major donors, awarded 3.2 million dollars for tuition assistance this past year. Funds were also allocated for marketing/public relations education and technology grants to individual schools. It is our hope that next year monies will be allocated for counseling in inner-city schools and an arts program.

An annual report is prepared for donors and students receiving assistance are requested to write letters of appreciation for inclusion. In some instances, individual corporations have established partnerships with specific schools.

Stewardship and development efforts for institutional advancement are well-established in a majority of secondary schools. The concepts are, however, new to elementary schools and data suggests that significant efforts are needed to educate parents and school personnel around the meaning and reasons for comprehensive development planning. Resources are available from the NCEA, from diocesan development offices, educational consultants, books, periodicals and software programs.

If we truly believe that our schools are gifts to society, we are challenged to tell our story and to recognize that some things are not accomplished without the active participation of the entire school community. This points up a central emphasis of Christian stewardship.

From the standpoint of human capacity to serve, persons are entrusted with a variety of resources including time, material things and human abilities. These are provided in order that each person may have a part in the achievement of God's purposes. Let us be partners with God in furthering the Kingdom and the mission of quality Catholic education.

Question Five

We heard very clearly from several groups about the importance of pursuing educational vouchers. What are the issues surrounding vouchers that we need to examine and be prepared to address?

Respondent: Lourdes Sheehan, RSM, executive director, Department of Chief Administrators of Catholic Education, NCEA

First of all, let me say that I am a firm believer in parental choice in education. That choice can and should take various forms of which vouchers are but one type. Another conviction of mine is that all parents, including those who choose private and religious schools for their children, are entitled to a fair share of their tax dollar.

One of the first issues which needs to be addressed is dispelling the many myths that opponents offer to publicly-funded voucher or scholarship opportunities legislation. They suggest that any type of voucher plan will take money away from the "poor" public schools. We need to counter that the money is the public's money and that the public should have a say in how the funds are allocated.

Another issue, already addressed in legislative efforts, relates to what compromises are religious schools able and willing to accept. The most obvious concerns of most Catholic school administrators surround admission policies and attendance in formal religion classes and worship services.

Many Catholic school administrators who accept students with privately funded scholarships already face the dilemma of how to cover the difference between the amount of tuition charged and the scholarship offered. In most instances, the scholarship does not pay the full cost of educating the student because the stated tuition is often not the per-pupil cost.

Already 41% of Catholic schools report waiting lists for admission and new schools are not being built fast enough to accommodate the population growths in many areas. I believe that major concerns will emerge around the issue of balancing the expansion needed in many areas with the reorganizing and merging of schools in other sections. Where dioceses and archdioceses will choose to put their resources will be a significant issue as more parents have a choice to select a private or religious school for their children's education.

Editor's Note:

Additional voucher issues related to the challenges that we will face when a voucher law is enacted were identified by Dr. Leonard DeFiore, president of the National Catholic Educational Association, at its annual meeting in April 1999 in New Orleans. They are the following:

- What is the impact of a lottery and financial-need-driven eligibility process on the task of developing and maintaining community within a school and parish? Given the importance we attach to community and its effectiveness, we need to find effective ways to cope with what may be negative forces in these circumstances.

- What are some of the administrative "temptations" which might arise with the prospect of a voucher, which exceeds current tuition practices? Might a pastor or school board be tempted to solve many of its school's financial problems by jumping tuition to the maximum rate allowed as soon as possible?

- Is there a need for guidance statements for tuition practices and other financial issues that prevent counterproductive practices and subsequent negative perceptions about vouchers and schools?

- Do Catholic schools need a contingency plan for expanding their capacity to accommodate more students who will seek to enroll if a voucher is available?
- Is there a need to develop financial models for schools that provide us with the ability to disengage from a voucher program and remain fiscally sound should circumstances require us to do so? This may be necessary if, several years into the voucher program, a requirement were added with which we could not abide, for example, students' participation in religion class must be optional or forbidden altogether. How does the school retain the option to withdraw and remain financially viable?

Question Six

All of us have been faced with the challenge to increase enrollment and to pay higher salaries. How can we redesign Catholic education to accomplish more with less money?

Respondent: Brother Robert R. Bimonte, FSC, vicar and superintendent, Diocese of Buffalo, New York

The National Catholic Educational Association's data report that overall we continue to meet the challenge to increase enrollment. For the last six years enrollment has increased by 81,000 students. Thirty-six schools opened this year, which brings the number to 200 new schools that opened over the last 10 years.[1] Even though nationwide enrollment has increased, it may be a challenge for some individual schools. Contrary to some belief, the students enrolled in our Catholic schools do not come from rich families. According to Michael Guerra, executive director of the NCEA Secondary Department, a significant number of secondary students come from working class and middle-income families.[2]

Paying salaries that are just continues to be a priority, yet a challenge, for administrators and boards of education. How do we stretch the dollar to pay teachers more and at the same time expand services/programs to eliminate factors that inhibit students' learning? Catholic schools have enjoyed a fine reputation for doing a lot with less money. Maybe the question is not how they can be redesigned to do more with less, but how can they be redesigned to meet the many needs of youth and their families of today for less?

The 1997 SPICE program focused on that issue. Twelve programs showcased various Catholic school partnerships that enable the school to provide services that they could not offer alone because of lack of human and financial resources. The programs include reorganizing six urban elementary schools on Chicago's westside to provide full-service programs for the students and their families to a multi-faceted program staffed by the Sisters of Charity of St. Elizabeth that provides services to a diverse immigrant community of which the schools are a part. All the programs are described in the publication, *Conversations in Excellence: Creatively Meeting the Needs of Youth and Their Families.*[3]

Use of technology is another way that Catholic schools could do more for less, for example, a language teacher could teach French simultaneously at several other schools.

The people who create and direct these programs have broken down the idea of "parochial" in the negative sense. These programs point out that Catholic schools are not self-sufficient. Schools need to partner with other parishes, other schools and agencies, such as Catholic Charities, USA, Catholic Social Services and Catholic hospitals to educate the whole child.

Respondent: Dr. Jerome Porath, superintendent of schools, Archdiocese of Los Angeles

The traditional challenge for Catholic school principals, like other financial managers, has been either to increase revenues or to decrease expenses. With Catholic schools known for their low operational costs (and great tuition values for parents), further cost reductions are unlikely. If anything, costs ought to increase to raise teacher compensation.

Others have talked about raising additional revenue through new tuition programs, development efforts or additional services that offer new revenue streams. But there may be another alternative: redesigning schools.

The opportunity may exist (everyone must be careful to recognize that this is a possibility, not a proven fact) to offer educational services using recently available technology at lower cost. This would occur if technologically delivered instruction significantly altered the pupil-teacher ratios. If teachers facilitated the learning process for larger groups of students, the savings in compensation costs could more than pay for the expenses of hardware and software.

"Redesign" is more than having students learn from a computer or from videos. It requires some new thinking about an old idea. The old idea is individual instruction; the new thinking involves getting the right mix of instruction delivered from the new technologies, from an individual tutor-teacher and from interaction with other students. If such a "redesign" happens, Catholic schools may be able to educate their students at a lower cost.

Conclusion

The panelists presented their thinking on the themes that surfaced during the many conversations that took place at the symposium. The themes are leadership, alternative development models, redesigning Catholic education to accomplish more with less, basic assumptions about Catholic schools, stewardship of financial gifts and issues surrounding vouchers. Because the panel was last on the agenda, time prevented the participants from engaging in a long conversation with the panelists about each theme. So we pass these questions onto you, the readers of this book, to continue the dialogue. I am confident that from the exchange will flow many ideas that will lead to creative financing and resourcing of Catholic schools.

Endnotes

1   Dale McDonald, PBVM, *United States Catholic Elementary and Secondary Schools 1998–1999* (Washington, DC: National Catholic Educational Association, 1999).

2   Michael Guerra, *CHS2000: A First Look* (Washington, DC: National Catholic Educational Association, 1998)

3   Regina Haney and Joseph O'Keefe, SJ, *Conversations in Excellence: Providing for the Diverse Needs of Youth and their Families* (Washington, DC: National Catholic Educational Association, 1997).

Presenters and Authors

SPICE Co-Directors

Carol Cimino, SSJ, is director of the Catholic School Administrators Association of New York State.

Regina M. Haney is executive director of the National Association of Boards of Catholic Education.

Joseph M. O'Keefe, SJ, is associate professor of education at Boston College. For the 1999-2000 academic year, he is Visiting Associate Professor and holder of the Jesuit Chair at Georgetown University

Other Presenters and Authors

Robert R. Bimonte, FSC, is vicar and superintendent of schools in the Diocese of Buffalo, New York.

Lee Brennan is vice president of Chase Manhattan Bank in Princeton Junction, Jew Jersey.

Francis J. Butler is president of Foundations and Donors Interested in Catholic Activities (FADICA) in Washington, DC.

Lawrence S. Callahan is superintendent of schools in the Archdiocese of Washington, DC.

Timothy W. Dwyer is superintendent of schools in the Diocese of Rochester, New York.

Daniel J. Elsener is executive director of the Christel Deltaan Family Foundation in Indianapolis, Indiana.

Howard Gray, SJ, is director of the Center for Ignatian Spirituality at Boston College.

Joseph Claude Harris of Seattle, Washington, is a consultant and noted expert on Catholic school finance.

Peter Lynch is vice chairman of Fidelity Management and Research Company, a trustee of the Fidelity Group of Funds, and former manager of the Fidelity Magellan Fund. A graduate of Boston College, the highly successful financier, consultant and speaker often contributes his expertise to the cause of Catholic education.

Dale McDonald, PBVM, is director of public policy and education research at National Catholic Educational Association (NCEA).

Jerome R. Porath is superintendent of schools in the Archdiocese of Los Angeles, California.

Ann Dominic Roach, OP, is superintendent of schools in the Archdiocese of Boston, Massachusetts.

Lourdes Sheehan, RSM, is secretary of education at the United States Catholic Conference. At the time of the conference, she was executive director of the NCEA Department of Chief Administrators of Catholic Education.

Michael Skube is superintendent in the Diocese of Charlotte, North Carolina.

Mary E. Tracy, SNJM, is associate executive director of the NCEA Department of Secondary Schools.

Acknowledgements and Sponsors

Acknowledgements

Selected Programs for Improving Catholic Education could not exist without the efforts of many generous people. The SPICE Committee that prepared the 1998 Conversations in Excellence conference deserves recognition. Along with co-directors Carol Cimino, SSJ; Regina Haney and Joseph O'Keefe, SJ, were CACE representatives Robert Bimonte, FSC; Lawrence Bowman; Michael Skube and Lourdes Sheehan, RSM (executive director of CACE at the time). Representing the Division of Supervision, Personnel and Curriculum of CACE were Annette Lentz (director of education in the Archdiocese of Indianapolis) and Barbara Swanson (associate superintendent in the Diocese of Jefferson City, Missouri). Representing NCEA were Leonard DeFiore (president); Mary Frances Taymans, SND (associate executive director of the Department of Secondary Schools); and Antoinette Dudek, OSF (executive director for early childhood and special education services of the Department of Elementary Schools).

Sponsors

Funding for *Conversations in Excellence 1998* came from a variety of resources and is gratefully acknowledged.

Corporate gifts came from:

William H. Sadlier, Inc.

Paulist Press

Our Sunday Visitor, Inc.

SMART Tuition Management Services

F.A.C.T.S. Management Company

P.L.A.T.O. Junior

Catholic School Management, Inc.

Grants were provided by:

The Father Michael J. McGivney Memorial Fund for New Initiatives in Catholic Education

The Chief Administrators of Catholic Education Research Center Board

Financial and human resources from Boston College were provided by:

The Peter and Caroline Lynch School of Education

The Jesuit Institute

The Jesuit Community

CONVERSATIONS IN EXCELLENCE ORDER FORM

Complete this order form and mail

SPICE

PREPAID/CREDIT
CARD order to:

BILLED order to:

NCEA
Publication Sales
P.O. Box 0227
Washington,D.C. 20055

NCEA
Publication Sales
Suite 100
1077 30th Street, N.W.
Washington,D.C. 20007-3852

or Tel: 202-337-6232; Fax: 202-333-6706; E-mail: pubs@ncea.org

Name _____ Tel Number _____

Title _____

Institution _____

Address _____

City/State/Zip _____

Credit card: ____MasterCard ____Visa

____Payment enclosed

Card Number _____

____Bill me

Date of Expiration _____

____Credit Card
Only orders in excess of $25
may be billed.

Name on Card _____

Signature _____

	Quantity	Amount
Conversations in Excellence		
NEW! Creatively Financing & Resourcing $17 member/$22 nonmember	_____	_____
Providing for Diverse Needs $16 member/$20 nonmember	_____	_____
Integrating the Mission $12 member/$16 nonmember	_____	_____
Special price for all three books $39 member/$51 nonmember	_____	_____
Add shipping/handling		$ 4.00
Total	_____	_____

____Sign me up as a subscriber to the NCEA Publications Standing Order Service (SOS). I understand that I will receive, with a bill, new NCEA publications that sell for $20 or less. NCEA will pay postage and handling.